CREATIVE
NONFICTION

8

Mostly Memoir

CREATIVE NONFICTION 8

Editor
Lee Gutkind

Managing Editor
Leslie Boltax Aizenman

Business Manager
Patricia Park

Production Editor
Debra Zarecky

Assistant Editor
Jessica Rohrbach

Copy Editor
Debra Zarecky

Online Editor
Larry Bielawski

Editorial Advisory Board
Laurie Graham
Patricia Park
Lea Simonds

Two excerpts contained in "An Album Quilt" by John McPhee were originally published in different form in The New Yorker as "Opening the Stacks" ©1993 and "Remembering Mr. Shawn" ©1992. An excerpt appeared in Lady's Choice published by the University of New Mexico Press.

Address correspondence, unsolicited material, subscription orders and other queries to The Creative Nonfiction Foundation, 5501 Walnut St., Suite 202, Pittsburgh, PA 15232. Telephone: 412-688-0304; Fax: 412-683-9173; e-mail: lgu+@pitt.edu; Internet: http://www.goucher.edu/~cnf. Manuscripts will not be returned unless accompanied by a self-addressed, stamped envelope.

Creative Nonfiction (ISSN #1070-0714) is distributed in the U.S. by Ingram Periodicals Inc., 1240 Heil Quaker Blvd., La Vergne, TN 37068-7000, 800-627-6247; B. DeBoer, Inc., 113 East Center Street, Nutley, NJ 07110, 201-667-9300; and Desert Moon Periodicals, 1226 Calle de Comercio, Santa Fe, NM 87505, 505-474-6311. Creative Nonfiction is indexed in the American Humanities Index (Whitston Publishing Company).

Contents

Special appreciation to Goucher College and the Center for Graduate and Continuing Studies for support for this "Mostly Memoir" issue.

ₑ

*The Creative Nonfiction Foundation
also gratefully acknowledges
the **Juliet Lea Hillman Simonds Foundation, Inc.**
for its ongoing support
and
the **Lila Wallace-Reader's Digest Fund**.*

ₑ

The Creative Nonfiction Foundation wishes to acknowledge the contributions of the following "Friends" whose generous donations make the publication of this journal possible:

Linda Berganske

W. Dieter Bergman

Larry Bielawski

Laurie A. Birnsteel

Douglas Black

Alice D. Bloch

Ellen Brodsky

Terri Butler

Gene Calvert

Jeanne DeMars

John Hartsock

Megan LeBoutiller

Patricia Levinson

Gigi Marino

George R. Merrill

Linda Needleman

Sue Nirenberg

Carolyn Olbum

Michael Perry

Fazlur Rahman, M.D.

Lisa Richesson

Barbara Rosof

Mimi Schwartz

Norman Sims

Warren Slesinger

Louisa Smyth

Jeff Unger

David Van Ness Taylor

From the Editor
Anatomy of "An Album Quilt" Excerpt
Lee Gutkind

*T*his issue was inspired by the first annual Mid-Atlantic Creative Nonfiction Summer Writers' Conference sponsored by Creative Nonfiction and Goucher College in Baltimore, Md. As Creative Nonfiction is the only literary magazine to publish nonfiction exclusively, so, too, was this event the only conference to feature workshops, readings, seminars and panels about nonfiction, only.

For six days last August, writers from as far away as Alaska studied and dialogued with some of the most energetic and accomplished nonfiction writers, including Diane Ackerman ("A Natural History of the Senses"), Darcy Frey ("The Last Shot"), Washington Post columnist Jeanne Marie Laskas and Paul West ("My Mother's Music"). There were editors and literary agents, as well.

There was also John McPhee.

I say this in a single line because McPhee's work and his ongoing impact on the creative nonfiction community deserve singular attention. They symbolize exactly what creative nonfiction represents—the classic 5 Rs I have often discussed, including reportage, reflection, research, real life—and high-quality prose ('riting). McPhee's essays in The New Yorker or his two dozen books ("Coming Into the Country," "Looking for a Ship," etc.) are accurate and informational, yet enriched with the author's personal experiences and observations. Indeed, in most of McPhee's work, a reader is captivated by substance rather than persona; we feel McPhee's strong presence, but he does not call attention to himself unless absolutely necessary. In his 60,000-word book, "The Deltoid Pumpkin Seed," he uses the word "I" (in reference to himself) twice.

McPhee's work is distinguished by his ability to see the world through the points of view of other people and communicate them intricately and intimately.

The fact that McPhee participated in the conference at Goucher was significant; he is known to be somewhat reticent. Private and driven, McPhee will devote months or years researching books and essays, traveling the world. And when he is not in Switzerland, Russia, Fairbanks or on the high seas with the merchant marine, he situates himself for 10-hour days, six days a week in an office in Princeton, New Jersey, his hometown, writing. One term a year, he emerges from hibernation to teach a special class at Princeton for students interested in "The Literature of Fact." Some of his more accomplished former students include Richard Preston ("The Hot Zone") and Sheryl WuDunn and David Remnick, both winners of the Pulitzer Prize.

McPhee's preference that he remain a basically private person includes the dust jackets for his books—sans traditional author's photo—and appearances on camera. One significant exception is a 22-minute video The New Yorker produced for promotional purposes, in which some of its most prestigious writers (Ann Beattie, Mark Singer, Jamaica Kincaid) discussed the joys and challenges of writing for "the best magazine that ever was." The video is a delight. In one sequence, Roger Angell recalls the moment he discovered an unsolicited story by Garrison Keillor and charged out of his office and down the hallway, waving the manuscript triumphantly. But the highlight is McPhee, a bearded grisly-looking character with a gravelly voice and a self-effacing manner, closeted in a drab, low-ceilinged room, like a mole. McPhee admits the typical writer's dilemma: procrastination. Just because he is in his office day after day, "certainly doesn't mean I am working ... I just walk around, make a cup of coffee or tea, look out the window, inventing ways to avoid writing ... until 4 or 5 p.m. comes along, and it is really getting to be late, and then I'll get going. If I have a good day I might actually be writing four hours, tops."

I had never met McPhee, and I was surprised to discover how outgoing and articulate he was, compared to what I had often heard about his elusiveness. Then came Goucher, at which McPhee presented a truly magnificent reading, partially culled from his book, "Rising From the Plains" (1986), which included numerous unpublished excerpts from the journals of Ethel Waxham, who came to Wyoming at the turn of the century to teach in a one-room schoolhouse. McPhee's wife, Yolanda Whitman, joined him in the presentation, reading all of Waxham's journal entries and quotations. The following day, McPhee arrived on campus in the early afternoon and participated in a public dialogue about his methods of research, interviewing, etc.—an event that went on, basically nonstop, for more than five hours.

According to McPhee, "Writing begets writing. You feel yourself growing as the result of the writing you do." Normally, he will write four drafts of essays, and he reads everything he writes aloud before the final draft. McPhee revealed that his objective at the beginning of each essay or book—his first official writing act—is "to find a good way into the piece, a lead," he said, "that works; a lead that isn't cheap; a lead that shines down into the subject and illuminates it. Almost always, I know the last line of the piece before I know anything else." Interestingly, McPhee admitted that even in his advanced writing career, he starts the first draft of an essay or book with absolutely "no confidence."

McPhee's work has inspired my own nine nonfiction books. His adventures and discoveries in "The Pine Barrens" were especially influential early in my career, and, later on, "Heirs of General Practice" helped ease me into the world of medicine. In the course of our conversations at Goucher, he told me about a past and future project of his, a montage he called "An Album Quilt."

A few years ago, he began putting together his writing that had never been published in book form—or published at all. This included articles from his earliest days at Time and a number of unsigned pieces written for the "Talk of the Town" section of The New Yorker. It also included random, unpublished notes, about 250,000 words in all, which McPhee refined into about 75,000. His aim, he explained, was not merely to reproduce and reprint, "but to present a montage of patches and fragments of past work that I have picked out and cut and trimmed (and edited and touched-up in the minor ways that I would edit and touch-up the final draft of any new piece

of writing) and sewn together as if it were an album quilt."
Developed in Baltimore in the 1840s, album quilts were custom-
made for individuals, and often commemorated technological inno-
vations but also dealt with personal histories.

"The items in the montage are not adorned with titles,"
McPhee explained, "but are separated only by very small line draw-
ings of individual quilt patches. In the paragraph of general intro-
duction, however, mention will be made of a combination of notes,
bibliography and table of contents that will be found at the end of
the book. It will include topics, notes, page numbers and anything
else I feel I ought to say about the nature and origin of each item.
A browsing reader can look there and pick out Richard Burton or
Woody Allen or Barbra Streisand or Oscar Robertson and see the
number of the page on which the relevant item begins. Sources will
appear there, with dates." McPhee explained that "An Album Quilt,"
although considerably altered and rearranged, was still a draft; he and
his longtime friend and publisher Roger Straus (Farrar, Straus and
Giroux) had discussed publication sometime in the future, a few
years hence. Meanwhile, he asked, would I care to read it?

Some months went by until we actually settled back into our
respective offices and McPhee was able to locate a copy of "An
Album Quilt" and send it off. For the next week, I set aside an hour
a day, tucked "Quilt" under my arm, and walked up the street to my
favorite coffee shop to read. The experience was fulfilling—on a
number of levels. In reading "An Album Quilt," I discovered some
old, unsigned favorites I hadn't seen for many years, such as the "Talk
of the Town" piece about the poor, absentminded professor
(McPhee) who locks his keys in his car in downtown Manhattan
near the Fulton Fishmarket. There are profiles of Mort Sahl, Joan
Baez, Jackie Gleason, the latter two beginning with classic descriptions (identities withheld) which capture the essence of the subjects
with bell-ringing clarity, along with Marion Davies, Richard
Rodgers, Cary Grant. Aside from the notion that this was pure, ter-
rific, original McPhee, which is the standard of excellence in the
creative nonfiction/literary journalism field today, the real joy in
reading "An Album Quilt" was the fact that each turn of the page
offered another unpredictable, delightful surprise.

Some of the jewels of "An Album Quilt" are contained in the more personal entries, mostly unpublished, which capture the warm and intimate qualities that I discovered when I first met McPhee, face to face, at Goucher. In fact, as I read through "An Album Quilt" (twice) at my coffee shop, I earmarked a half-dozen of these pieces as "special" because they illuminated a heretofore veiled, personal side of McPhee. I approached McPhee about publishing these pieces which, I am happy to say, appear in this issue.

As you will see, McPhee writes of his home state, New Jersey, and the six Princetons he perceives; we meet his children and son-in-law, accomplished and worldly characters like their father; we learn more about the Ethel Waxham journal; and we meet his good friends and colleagues, William Shawn and Roger Straus, who inspired and supported him. I've lifted these jewels from 75,000 words of delightfully disordered spontaneity to be the centerpiece of Creative Nonfiction's eighth issue—our largest ever, 12 essays in all. McPhee's New Yorker colleague, Alec Wilkinson, is also included in this issue, as well as essayist Phillip Lopate, poets Donald Morrill and Kathryn Rhett, whose first nonfiction books will soon be published by Duquesne University Press' Emerging Writers in Creative Nonfiction book series, and novelist Ellen Gilchrist, who notes in the bio to her essay that she is currently, among other projects, "re-reading the works of John McPhee."

Meanwhile, the Mid-Atlantic Creative Nonfiction Summer Writers' Conference which McPhee helped launch last year has been scheduled for August 12-16, 1997, in Baltimore, featuring readings, workshops and discussions with a number of other prestigious nonfiction writers, including Tracy Kidder, Tobias Wolff, Gay Talese, Lauren Slater, Darcy Frey, Jeanne Marie Laskas, Susan Orlean—and me. Hope to see you there. For information, call 1-800-697-4646.

Lee Gutkind's next book of creative nonfiction, "An Unspoken Art" (Henry Holt and Company), deals with animals, animal lovers and their veterinarians.

At a Turn in the Road

Lucy Wilson Sherman

*T*here we were, taking the long way home through the park, Toby, my black lab, bounding on ahead, doing two miles for every one of ours. Lovers we were, holding hands when we weren't struggling single file over rocks and roots. Lovers, inhaling the autumn afternoon, conscious only of the tromp and slide and crunch of our footsteps—and the silence. Lovers. Hardly killers.

The path narrowed so that one of us would hold the branch for the other, until gradually the path, once a logging road, now weedy and rocky from disuse, widened to the width of a car. And there, quietly edging upon our consciousness, was a car facing us in the turn of the road, with its motor running.

At a moment like this you become embarrassed, feeling as if you've been discovered at something. Discovered just being unself-conscious, maybe. You pull yourself out of your reverie, out of your private joke. You think: Damn people, intruding upon our afternoon, our privacy. Then you're embarrassed for whomever you're going to come upon. You think: Lovers maybe, necking, or more. You think: Oh, someone's just gone to take a leak. You think: Maybe there's a dead body in the front seat.

You prepare your face.

Your lover takes the left side of the car, and you take the right, the branches and tall weeds forcing you to pass close to the car. It's an old, gray, nondescript car, four doors, some rust along the fender you can see out of the corner of your eye. Of course you try not to look, but the car is running, and you glance in as you brush past sideways.

There's a body, a guy on the front seat, curled up fetal fashion, asleep. So, he's got a right. But the car is running. You think: He's gonna suffocate, no windows open, car running—he'll be dead before he wakes. You look over the roof of the car at Rob, who hasn't given in to curiosity, who hasn't looked.

And now you're behind the car, and you glance back and see the hose attached to the tail pipe, and, by God, just like in some movie, just the way it would be in that movie we've all seen in our heads, the hose goes around on Rob's side, and you say, "Rob," who has passed by now, and your heart is pumping with excitement (this is real life) and fear, and you follow the hose around to the other side of the car, and sure enough, the hose goes into the front door, and you realize what's happening, and again, urgently, you say, "Rob," and finally he turns and sees.

So you realize there's a guy in there who has hooked up a hose to the tail pipe of his car, and the hose enters the front door and—he's doing it. He's actually doing it, just as you imagine when you hear how people kill themselves in their garages by turning on their cars and waiting. You've pictured yourself doing it. Well, by God, there's a guy doing it right out here in our park, broad daylight, well, afternoon, a glorious afternoon, your much-needed afternoon with Rob, unself-consciously melding with nature, and suddenly all your nerve endings are standing at attention, and you're sharp and distinct from the bushes and trees, and you think you should do something. Deal with this. You want to enter the drama but simultaneously resent that it has upstaged your own private, low-keyed, small, lover drama.

I have to enter the drama. I have to open the door. There's a temptation, a pull, a seductiveness to be in the presence of someone who's actually doing it. I want to see what it's like, although I'm scared now. Someone who's actually doing it is scary. Maybe it's done already, but then just seeing death is scary.

My hand is on the door, and now I've opened the door, stepping back quickly into the bushes. Fear makes me sound angry.

"Hey, what are you doing? What's going on here?" I sound like a cop.

Slowly, groggily, the guy lifts his head. He's alive, although his pale eyes looking up into my face are clouded, unfocused. He's youngish, probably Irish, with stringy, reddish-blond hair, a blond mustache. He looks like someone I would know.

"Leave me alone," he mumbles.

"Well, I can't, you see," I answer nervously, with a little laugh, just as if we're having this perfectly natural conversation. Toby's worrying a stick to death over near Rob.

"Go on away. Leave me alone." He's struggling to prop himself up on the steering wheel. It's a struggle, not only because he was on his way out, but because his gut is wedged in by the wheel.

"What are you doing, buddy?" Now I sound overly jovial. Rob has finally come back, but because he's still standing a little way off, as if about to run, I feel he must know something. His glasses are winking in the sun; I cannot see his eyes. Maybe somehow I've spoiled our afternoon by having to look. Maybe Rob is angry. Now I'm torn. This guy doesn't want me, and Rob wants to go home. He keeps shuffling, hands stuffed into the pockets of his jeans, shoulders hunched. He keeps glancing toward the paved road. It's silent here in the park except for this shuffling, the thrum of the car motor and Toby still humbling that stick. There's no one else around, and we can't see the main road from here. I think maybe I've created this.

"What are you doing?" I can't seem to think of anything else to say. He's looking straight ahead, up the path further into the woods, one arm hanging onto the steering wheel for support, thick, nicotine-yellowed fingers (he's a lefty) tapping on the dash, no wedding ring. Then I see the case of Budweiser on the floor in the back, crumpled cigarette packs and some dirty laundry on the seat.

"Why so much beer?" There are empties tossed onto the floor in the front, and his cigarette is still lit in the ash tray. There's something forlorn about that cigarette burning, waiting to be dragged on, life going on.

"It's for the people who find me." His words are slurred. "So they can have a real party when they find me. Now shut the door and leave me alone."

That part about the people who'll find him drinking his case of beer ticks me off. I shift my weight and look at Rob.

"Rob, what'll I do?"

"Get his keys."

"Aw, shit, just shut the fucking door. Get the fuck away from me."

More minutes of silence while I look back and forth between the guy and Rob. The guy stares out the front window, fully upright now. Rob is impatient. He shuffles a little farther from the car, a little closer to the main road. I think, this guy means business. I picture wailing sirens, cop cars, flashing lights, the ambulance, all that noise breaking into this guy's final moments. This thing he's doing is as private as masturbation. This guy is serious, and I am timid before him. I have never done anything so deadly serious. Now I am moved. I do not want the cops with their sirens and stretchers and their loud bullying voices to disrespect this man and rush him unwilling to a hospital and pump out his stomach, or whatever they do for carbon monoxide poisoning, and treat him as if he doesn't mean it. I am sobered. This is no joke. I think he means it.

And I have no words of hope for him. I have my own problems and my own doubts. What he's doing makes me want to glance behind me, over my shoulder, as if he knows something about life I don't. As if he's leaving a bad party and by leaving makes me see how dreary it really is. What's so great about taking a walk in the park with your supposed lover? I mean, it doesn't solve anything. Nothing at all. It's irrelevant, really, when you consider all the times in life when things go wrong. This party stinks.

If Rob were not here, I know what I would do. I would gently close the door on the hose, being careful not to shut off its supply of noxious gas. I would raise my hands, palms forward, to show I meant no harm, and, crouching, I would back away.

"Keys. Get his keys," says Rob, suddenly efficient, crisp, though still standing down the road, out of the guy's sight.

His words galvanize me, and now it becomes a game: Will I dare to reach in past the guy (maybe death will grab me too) and pull his keys out of the ignition? That will spoil it for him, inconvenience him, when, after all, if he's gone to this length, he's probably been troubled enough in life.

"We'll put the keys at the end of the road. That'll give him time to think it over." Rob has it figured out now.

"But I don't want to inconvenience him." Rob and I are talking the way you do in front of a child. We're talking as if he's already dead.

"Tell her to shut the door, Rob." He's heard me call Rob's name. "What the fuck do you think you're doing? Both of you, leave me alone." His voice is weary. I understand.

"I'm sorry, but I have to do this."

"Get the fuck away. I've got something in the back seat that'll make you get away." He straightens up, his left hand on the steering wheel, his right arm over the back of the seat.

Oh, shit, what's he mean, "something." A gun, under all those clothes? This man, so free with his own life, would not have the usual compunction.

Quickly, I reach in and pull the keys out of the ignition, thinking if they stick, he'll grab my arm and pull me into where he's going. But they don't stick, and I get them and start backing away, apologizing.

"Aw, shit, what are you gonna do with my keys?"

High on my courage, I run to catch up with Rob, whose long legs are carrying him toward the road at a great rate. He calls back, "We'll leave them at the end of the road. You'll have to come and get them, see?" And to me he says, "This will give him time to get some air and think it over."

"How will I find them?" the guy yells. I turn to Rob, who seems to have done this many times before, so sensible is his idea, whereas I just wanted us to figure out a way not to inconvenience the guy, to leave him with his dignity.

"We'll leave them on," (we're striding away now and calling back, and then Rob sees a beer can) "on a beer can." (How fitting.)

"What?"

We do it. Set the empty can on end in the tall weeds and carefully place the keys so he can see the can and the keys when he gets here.

I shout, wanting to be helpful, "They're on a beer can."

And then we start up the main road. Toby abandons his stick when we call. We leash him now and quicken our steps. After all, anything can happen—he could be hit by a car—we want him close to us. Death is breathing down our necks.

As we reach the top of the hill, we hear, "Rob, where're the keys?"

I turn, see him, and make exaggerated motions toward the can, wanting to be helpful. It's all I can do now. I want him to know we care. We want him to have a good experience. At least that's the way it is for me. Rob and I are not talking now, just high-tailing it home.

We think he finds the keys. There is silence again; it has closed over behind us.

To Rob I say, breathless, "I don't want to call the police. I believe a person should be allowed to make this decision."

I believe in suicide. I believe in death with dignity, and I believe each person ultimately knows his own course—at least we must operate on that premise. When I'm old or sick, I want a pill. And when I die, I'd like my family around me. I'll take the pill with all of them there, so they can watch, so they won't be so afraid for themselves. We were at my mother's bedside when she took her last three breaths. We watched and wept, but it was good to see. Her dying then became a part of my life, and now I am not so afraid. Only, I want to say when.

I am exhilarated. The adrenaline is pumping through my very alive body. We march home quickly as evening comes on.

"I don't want to call the cops, Rob."

He does not protest, and I, proud I have stuck by my principles, which were only words before, do not open myself to their challenge and possible overthrow.

I am saddened by what has happened. I did not know I would decide like this. I thought surely my heart would bleed. The rush I used to get from rescuing people has diminished over the years, as I begin to save myself.

I am too charged to eat dinner. We talk about it; we tell my daughter, Amy. Neither Rob nor Amy says, "Let's call the police." Perhaps I present the story in such a way that they see it my way. They agree that, by God, he got as far off the road as he could—he really didn't want us to find him and stop him. We shouldn't have happened along. "The guy intruded on our afternoon," says Rob, almost shouting. I think he's nervous, but I really don't know. He does not discuss his feelings.

We wonder if we could be said to be accomplices. We talk in hushed voices without turning on the light over the dining room table. Maybe, with the breath of fresh air, he won't do it. After all, who do we know who really means business, who sticks by what they believe. Life is so lukewarm; you are so little called upon to put your money where your mouth is. You can get by in a half-life without ever taking a stand or even being fully awake. You can hedge and compromise. There's so much wasted time in life, so many unaccounted-for hours, so much dross. And here's this guy doing it. He has stature, in my eyes, integrity, calling it quits when it's no good anymore, rather than selling out, biding his time until death taps him.

I do not ask myself, is his despair only momentary? Is it merely a transient state that I should wheedle him out of? Or an inverted act of aggression which I have a responsibility to stop? I do not ask myself these things, and it is only many years later that it occurs to me that these beliefs I am so proud of may have blinded me to the particularities of the man before me. In taking for granted that this man's action was deliberate and considered, and grew out of his principles, I was making the solipsistic assumption that he was no different from me.

I prepare for bed, a clear purposefulness to my actions. Each motion is precise, distinct from every other motion. I pay attention to what I'm doing and wonder if it's worth it. That is, what it is he knows that I only suspect. His choosing death has brought me closer to the narrow edge of my own life, and I wonder if he doesn't have a point.

The next morning, without a word between us, we know we want to go back and see. I'm rooting for him to have done it, but I don't tell Rob that.

We retrace our path down the hill by car, and when we reach the dirt road, we see the car. Holy shit. This has the throb of reality. I'm always wondering when reality is going to kick in.

There are no sounds except Nature going on about her mindless business and the crunch of our footsteps on dry leaves as we creep up to just behind the car. There, with one quick look, we see him lying fetal fashion on the front seat. The hose is connected to the tailpipe and leads into the front door. The engine has run down.

We retreat fast and drive home. Now, now Rob calls the police. We make breakfast and wait. Then we hear sirens in the distance. He can't hear them now. It is over. I am shivering with exhilaration and awe and horror at myself. I feel proud of him, although I am aware that others might not applaud what he has done, what we have not done.

Lovers, we were, not killers. But not saviors either.

Lucy Wilson Sherman *is studying for her MFA in creative nonfiction at Goddard College in Vermont. "At a Turn in the Road" is one of a collection of personal essays (in progress) called "Uncommon Passions, Unnatural Acts." She lives with her husband on their 71-acre farm in Susquehanna, Pa.*

Like a Flower of Feathers
or a Winged Branch

Ellen Gilchrist

*T*his is Pedro Calderon de la Barca's description of a bluebird. I read this one morning in a doctor's office and have thought of it daily ever since. Every time I see a bird or a branch of leaves or a flower I think of it.

This is the job of writing, to carve indelible metaphors into the mind of a reader. Can't you see, the writer must tell the reader. It is all one thing. Look outside yourself and see that we are all fashioned of the same forms, the seven basic forms of crystals. Look outside yourself. Look at me.

If that is the task, how can the writer achieve it? I think it is like building a wall. Let us suppose that the beginning writer is a man living alone on a piece of land. He wants to build a wall to keep other people from coming onto his land, but he has no tools or knowledge. All he knows is that he wishes to construct a barrier. He collects what he finds lying around, leaves and fallen branches. He stacks these things up. The first wind blows them away.

He finds stones and begins to make piles of them, but they are heavy and cumbersome and in short supply so he soon gives that up. Then he travels to the next piece of land and finds a man who is making bricks out of clay and stacking them up. Our man likes that idea. He goes home and makes a wall of clay bricks, but the spring rains melt the bricks and the wall tumbles.

He meets a third man who is making bricks and letting them dry in the sun before he stacks them up. Our man is very excited by this idea. He goes home and works twice as hard as before. He doesn't care how hard it is to do, now he will make a wall that will hold.

As he works day after day and week after week fashioning the bricks and setting them out in the sun to dry, he begins to imagine a wall so beautiful that other men will come to see it and marvel at its beauty. He begins to make each brick exactly the same size, with sides carefully trimmed. He notices the clay from the banks of his creek makes more beautifully colored bricks than the clay near his campfire. He begins to make long trips to bring back this thicker, redder clay. Now he doesn't like the dun-colored bricks he made to begin with. He discards them. He is excited. He has lost his sense of time. He barely remembers to eat. He is going to make the most beautiful wall in the kingdom, the longest and the tallest and the most beautiful. Every day he gets up and works on the wall. He is a happy man. He has forgotten why he is building a wall. He has forgotten that he thought there was something that needed walling in or walling out. He is an artist with a plan and materials and skills. He has become a builder.

My life as a writer has been like that man making that wall. I have forgotten what I wanted from this work. I have never liked celebrity or having people ask me questions. Aside from being paid so I can go on writing, there is nothing the outside world gives me in exchange for my writing that is of value to me. I do not take pleasure in other people's praise, and I don't believe their criticism.

I love to make up characters and make things happen to them and then make them strong enough to survive their problems and go on to happy times. "Happy trails to you," I say to my characters at the end of my stories. I nearly always let my characters have happy endings because I wish that for myself and for my readers. I don't want to send my readers to bed with sad or malignant endings.

Pedro Calderon de la Barca lived in Spain in tragic times. His father was a tyrant, and the only woman he ever loved died in childbirth. She died giving birth to Calderon's illegitimate child. Because of these things Calderon was forced to have a tragic view of life. He was concerned with guilt. He believed that a man can be responsible through his own wrongdoing for the wrongdoing of another. That the greatest sinner is also the most sinned against. These are deeply tragic beliefs, and yet the poetry with which Calderon expressed these beliefs was so beautiful that it has lasted all these years.

Like a flower of feathers or a winged branch. That is what we want to write. But first we must learn to make a wall. We must find what materials are available to us, and we must learn to shape them, and we must forget what we were doing it for. If you get lonely, and it is lonely work, invoke the spirits of past artists to stand by you and teach you by their examples. Today, for me, it is Don Pedro Calderon de la Barca, poet and playwright, born January 17, 1600, Madrid, Spain, died, May 25, 1681, Madrid.

Ellen Gilchrist *lives in a stone and glass house built into the east-facing side of a hill in the Ozark Mountains. She reads and writes all day and is currently re-reading the works of John McPhee and worrying about the curve of binding energy. She has three grown sons and eight grandchildren. She has published 14 books. Her latest book is "The Courts of Love."*

The Story of My Father

Phillip Lopate

Is it not clearer than day, that we feel within ourselves the indelible marks of excellence, and is it not equally true that we constantly experience the effects of our deplorable condition?
—Pascal

Old age is a great leveler: The frailer elderly all come to resemble turtles trapped in curved shells, shrinking, wrinkled and immobile, so that, in a roomful, a terrarium of the old, it is hard to disentangle one solitary individual's karma from the mass fate of aging. Take my father. Vegetating in a nursing home, his character seems both universalized and purified, worn to its bony essence. But, as LSD is said to intensify more than alter one's personality, so old age: My father is what he always was, only more so. People meeting him for the first time ascribe his oddities (the withdrawn silences, sloppy eating habits, boasts and pedantic non sequiturs) to the infirmities of time, little realizing he was like that at 30.

A man in his 30s who acts the octogenarian is asking for it. But old age has set his insularities in a kinder light—meanwhile drawing to the surface that underlying sweetness that I always suspected was there. Dispassionate to the point where the stoical and stony meet, a hater of sentimentality, he had always been embarrassed by his affections; but now he lacks the strength even to suppress these leakages. I have also changed and am more ready to receive them. These last 10 years—ever since he was put away in old age homes—have witnessed more expressions of fondness than passed between us in all the years before. Now when I visit him, he kisses me on sight and, during the whole time we are together, stares at me greedily, as though with wonder that such a graying cub came from his loins. For my part, I have no choice but to love him. I feel a tenderness welling up, if only at the sight of the wreck he has become. What we were never able to exhibit when he had all his wits about him—that animal bond between father and son—is now the main exchange.

Yet I also suspect sentimentality; and so I ask myself, how valid is this cozy resolution? Am I letting both of us off the hook too quickly? Or trying to corner the market on filial piety, while the rest of my family continues mostly to ignore him? Who is, who was, this loner, Albert Lopate, neglected in a back ward? I look at the pattern of his 85 years and wonder what it all adds up to: failure, as he himself claims, or a respectable worker's life for which he has little to be ashamed, as I want to believe? We spend most of our adulthoods trying to grasp the meanings of our parents' lives; and how we shape and answer these questions largely turns us into who we are.

My father's latest idea is that I am a lawyer. The last two times I've visited him in the nursing home, he's expressed variations on this theme. The first time he looked up at me from his wheelchair and said, "So, you're successful—as a lawyer?" By my family's scraping-by standards, I'm a worldly success; and worldly success, to the mistrustful urban-peasant mind of my father, befogged by geriatric confusion, can only mean a lawyer.

Lawyers, I should add, are not held in the highest regard in my family. They are considered shysters: smooth, glib, ready to sell you out. You could say the same about writers. In hindsight, one reason I became a writer is that my father wanted to be one. An autodidact who started out in the newspaper trade, then became a factory-worker and, finally, a shipping clerk, he wrote poetry in his spare time, and worshipped Faulkner and Kafka. I enacted his dream, like the good son (or usurped it, like the bad son), which seems not to have made him entirely happy. So he turns me into a lawyer.

Not that my father's substitution is all that far-fetched. I had entered college a pre-law major, planning to specialize in publishing law. Secretly I yearned to be a writer, though I did not think I was smart enough. I was right—who is?—but bluff got the better of modesty.

The last time I visited my father, he said, "I know what you want to be. *Abogado*." He smiled at his ability to call up the Spanish word you see on storefronts in barrios, alongside *notario*. So this time I was not yet the successful attorney, but the teenage son choosing his vocation. Sometimes old people get stuck on a certain moment in the past. Could it be that his mental clock had stopped around

1961, right about the time of his first stroke, when he'd just passed 50 (my present age) and I was 17? *Abogado*. It's so characteristic of my father's attachment to language that a single word will swim up from the dark waters of dotage. Even before he became addled, he would peacock his vocabulary, going out of his way to construct sentences with polysyllabic words such as "concommitant" or "prevaricate." My father fingers words like mah-jongg tiles, waiting to play a good one.

Lately he has been reverting to Yiddish phrases, which he assumes I understand, though I don't. This return to the mother tongue is not accompanied by any revived interest in Judaism—he still refuses to attend the home's religious services—but is all part of his stirring the pot of language and memories one last time.

I arrive around noon, determined to bring him outside for a meal. My father, as usual, sits in the dining room, a distance apart from everyone else, staring down at his chin. There are a group of old ladies whom he manages to tantalize by neither removing himself entirely from their company, nor giving them the benefit of his full attention. Though he has deteriorated badly in recent years, he still remains in better shape than some, hence a "catch." One Irish lady in particular, Sheila, with a twinkle in her cataracted eye, is always telling me what a lovely man my father is. He pays her no attention whatsoever.

It was not always thus. A letter he dictated for my sister Leah in California, when he first came to this home, contained the passage: "There's a woman by the name of Sheila who seems to be attracted to me. She's a heavyset woman, not too bad-looking, she likes me a lot, and is fairly even-tempered. I'm not sure of my feelings toward her. I'm ambivalent." (Ambivalent is a favorite Albert Lopate word. Purity of heart is for simpletons.) "Should I pursue this more aggressively, or should I let things go along at a normal pace?" The last line strikes me as particularly funny, given my father's inveterate passivity (what would aggressive pursuit entail for him?) and the shortage of time left to these ancients.

It took me awhile to give up the hope that my father would find companionship, or at least casual friendship, in a nursing home. But the chances were slim: This is a man who never had nor made a friend for as long as I can remember. Secondly, "friendship" is a cuddly term that ill describes the Hobbesian enmity and self-centeredness among this tribe of old people.

"Don't push anything out of the window!" yells one old woman to another. "If anything's pushed out the window, it's going to be you!"

"I want to get out of here, I want to forget you, and I won't forget you unless I get out of this room!" yells the second.

"You dirty pig."

"You're one, too."

So speak the relatively sane ones. The ward is divided between two factions: those who, like my father, can still occasionally articulate an intelligent thought, and those with dementia, who scream the same incoherent syllables over and over, kicking their feet and rending the air with clawed hands. The first group cordially detests the second. *Meshugana*, crazy, my father dismisses them with a word. Which is why, desperately trying to stay on the right side of Alzheimer's, he has become panicked by forgetfulness.

Asked how he is, he responds with something like: "It worries me I'm losing my memory. We were discussing the all-star pitcher the Dodgers used to have. Koufax. I couldn't remember Koufax's first name. Ridiculous!" For a man who once had quiz-show recall, such lapses are especially humiliating. He has been making alphabetical lists of big words to retain them. But the mind keeps slipping, bit by bit. I had no idea there could be so many levels of disorientation before coming to rest at senility.

This time, he has forgotten we've made a lunch date and sits ready to eat the institutional tray offered him. In a way, I prefer his forgetting our date to his response a few years ago, when he would wait outside three hours before my arrival, checking his watch every 10 minutes. As usual, he is dressed too warmly, in a mud-colored, torn sweater, for the broiling summer day. (These shabby clothes seem to materialize from nowhere: Where does his wardrobe come from, and whatever happened to the better clothes we bought him? Theft is common in these establishments.)

I am in a hurry to wheel him outside today, before he becomes too attached to his meal—and before the atmosphere of the nursing home gets to me.

I kiss him on top of his pink head, naked but for a few white hairs, and he looks at me with delight. He is proud of me. I am the lawyer, or the writer—in any case, a man of accomplishment. In another minute, he will start introducing me to the women at the next table, "This is my son," as he has already done a hundred times before, and they will pour on the syrup about what a nice father I have, how nice I am to visit him (which I don't do often enough), and how alike we look. This time I start to wheel him out immediately, hoping to skip the routine, when Sheila croaks in her Irish accent, "Don'tcha say hello to me any more?" Caught in the act of denying my father the social capital a visitor might bring him, I go over and schmooze a bit.

Meanwhile, the muskrat-faced Miss Mojabi (in the caste division of this institution, the nursing staff is predominantly Pakistani, the attendants mainly black, and the upper management Orthodox Jewish) reminds me that I must "sign the form" to take legal responsibility for our outing. Were Armaggedon to arrive, these nurses would be waiting pen in hand for a release signature. Their harsh, officious manner makes me want to punch them. I temper my rage with the thought that they are adequate if not loving—that it was we, the really unloving, who abandoned him to their boughten care.

My father's nursing home, located in Washington Heights, is perched on the steepest hill in Manhattan. After straining to navigate the wheelchair downhill, fantasizing what would happen if I let the handlebars slip (careening Papa smashing into tree), I bring us to a Chinese-Cuban takeout place on Broadway, a hole in the wall with three formica tables. It's Sunday, everything else is closed, and there are limits to how far north I am willing to push him in the August heat. My father seems glad to have made it to the outside; he wouldn't mind, I'm sure, being wheeled to Riverdale. Still, he has never cared much about food, and I doubt if the fare's quality will register on him one way or the other.

After asking him what he would like, and getting an inconclusive answer, I order sesame chicken and a beef dish at the counter. He is very clear on one thing: ginger ale. Since they have none, I substitute Mountain Dew. Loud salsa music on the radio makes it hard to hear him; moreover, something is wrong with his false teeth, or he's forgotten to put in the bridge, and he speaks so faintly I have to ask him to repeat each sentence several times. Often I simply nod, pretending to have heard. But it's annoying not to understand, so as soon as he clears his throat—signaling intent to speak—I put my ear against his mouth, receiving communiqués from him in this misted, intimate manner.

From time to time, he will end his silence with an observation, such as, "The men here are better-looking than the women." I inspect the middle-aged Dominican patrons, indoor picnickers in their Sunday best—the men gray-templed and stout, wearing dark suits or brocaded shirts; the women in skirts, voluptuously rounded, made-up, pretty—and do not share his opinion, but nod agreement anyway. I sense he offers these impressions less to express his notion of reality than to show he can still make comments. Ten minutes later, another mysterious remark arrives, from left field, like the one about "abogado." I prefer this system of waiting for my father to say something, between long silences, rather than prying conversation out of him. If my wife Cheryl were here, she would be drawing him out, asking him about the latest at the nursing home, whether he had seen any movies on television, what he thought of the food, if he needed anything. And later, she would consider the effort a success: "Did you see how much better he got, the longer we spoke? He's just rusty because nobody talks to him. But he's still sharp mental-ly...." I'm glad she's not here to see me failing to keep the conversa-tional shuttlecock aloft.

You must have heard that corny idea: A true test of love is when you can sit silently next to the beloved, without feeling any pressure to talk. I have never been able to accomplish this feat with any woman, howsoever beloved, but I can finally do it with one human being: my father. After 50 years of frustration as this lockjawed man's son, I no longer look on his uncommunicativeness as problematic or wounding. Quite the contrary: In my book, he has at last earned the right to be as closemouthed as he wants, just as I have earned the right to stare into space around him, indulging my own fly-on-the-wall proclivities.

He eats, engrossed, engaged in the uneven battle between morsel and fork. With the plastic utensils they have given us, it is not easy for a man possessing so little remaining hand-strength to spear chicken chunks. So he wields the fork like a spoon to capture a piece, transport it to his mouth, and crunch down, one half dropping into his lap. Those dark polyester pants, already seasoned, absorb the additional flavor of sesame sauce. He returns to the plate with that morose, myopic glare which is his trademark. My wife, I know, would have helpfully cut up the pieces into smaller bits. Me, I prefer to watch him struggle. I could say in my defense that I am respecting his autonomy more by letting him work out the problem on his own. Or I could acknowledge some streak of cruelty for allowing him this fiasco. The larger truth is that I have become a fly on the wall, and flies don't use utensils.

Eventually, I too cut up everything on my father's plate. So we both arrive at the same point, my wife and I, but at differing rates. Cheryl sizes up a new situation instantly and sets about eliminating potential problems for others—a draft, a tipsy chair—as though all the world were a baby she needed to protect. My tendency is to adjust to an environment passively, like my father, until such time as it occurs to me to do what a considerate Normal Person (which I am decidedly not, I am a Martian) would do in these same circumstances: shut the window, cut up the old man's meat. My father is also from Mars. We understand each other in this way. He too approaches all matter as obdurate and mystifying.

My father drops some broccoli onto his lap. "Oh Al, how could you?" my mother would have cried out. "You're such a slob!" We can both "hear" her, though she is some eight miles downtown. As ever, he looks up sheepish and abashed, with a strangely innocent expression, like a chimp who knows it is displeasing its master but not why.

It gives me pleasure to spare him the expected familial reproach. "Eat it with your hands, Pop. It's OK," I tell him. Who can object to an old man picking up his food? Certainly not the Dominicans enjoying themselves at the next table. Many African tribes eat with their fingers. The fork is a comparatively recent innovation, from the late Middle Ages; Ethiopians still think that the fork not only harms the food's taste, imposing a metallic distance, but also spoils the sociability of each eater scooping up lentils and meat with soft porridgy bread from the common pot. Mayhap my father is a noble Ethiopian prince, mistransmigrated into the body of an elderly Jew? Too late: The tyranny of the fork has marked him, and he must steal "inadvertent" bits for his fingers' guilty pleasures.

I empathize with that desire to live in one's head, performing an animal's functions with animal absent-mindedness. Sometimes I too eat that way when I'm alone, mingling culinary herbs with the brackish taste of my fingers, in rebellious solidarity with his lack of manners. Socially, my older brother Hal and I have striven hard to project ourselves as the opposite of my father—to seem forceful, attentive, active and seductive. But I feel my father's vagueness, shlumpiness and mania for withdrawal inhabit me like a flu when no one is looking.

Across the street from the cafe, a drunken bum about 60 is dancing by himself on a park bench to Latin jazz. He has no shirt on, revealing an alkie's skinny frame, and he seems happy, moving to the beat with that uncanny, delayed rhythm of the stoned. I point him out as a potentially diverting spectacle to my father, who shows no interest. The drunk, in a curious way, reminds me of my dad: They're both functioning in a solipsistic cone.

Surrounded by "that thick wall of personality through which no real voice has ever pierced on its way to us," as Pater phrased it, each of us is, I suppose, to some degree a solipsist. But my father has managed to exist in as complete a state of solipsism as any person I have ever known. When he gets into an elevator, he never moves to the back, although by now he must anticipate that others will soon be joining him. Inconsiderateness? The word implies the willful hurting of others whose existence one is at least aware of.

I once saw an old woman in the nursing home elevator telling him to move back, which he did very reluctantly, and only a step at a time for each repeated command. (Perhaps, I rationalized for him, he has a faulty perception of the amount of space his body takes up.) The old woman turned to her orderly and said: "When you get on in years you have to live with old people. Some of them are nice and some are—peculiar." Meaning my father. When we got off the elevator he said, loudly: "She's such a pain in the ass, that one. Always complaining. I'll give her such a *luk im kopf*" (a smack in the head). His statement showed that he had been aware of her, but not enough to oblige her.

My father has always given the impression of someone who could sustain very little intensity of contact before his receptive apparatus shut down. Once, after I hadn't seen him in a year, I hugged him and told him how much I loved him. "OK, OK. Cut the bullshit," he said. This armor of impatience may have been his defense against what he actually wanted so much that it hurt.

"OK" is also his transitional marker, indicating he has spent long enough on one item and is ready for new data. If you haven't finished, so much the worse for you.

My sister Molly is the only one who can challenge his solipsism. She pays him the enormous compliment of turning a deaf ear to his self-pity and assuming that, even in old age, there is still potential for moral growth. Years ago, hospitalized with pneumonia, he was complaining to her that nobody cared enough to visit him, and she shot back: "Do you care about anyone? Are you curious about anyone besides yourself?" She then tried to teach him, as one would a child, how to ask after others' well-being. "When you see them, say: 'How are you? What have you been up to lately? How are you feeling?'" And for a while, it took. My father probably said "How are you?" more times between the ages of 75 and 79 than in all the years preceding. If the question had a mechanical ring, if he speedily lost interest in the person's answer, that ought not to detract from the worthiness of my sister's pedagogy.

My father's solipsism is a matter of both style and substance. When I was writing an essay on the Holocaust, I asked him if he had any memories of refugees returning from the camps. He seemed affronted, as though to say: Why are you bothering me with that crazy business afer all these years? "Ask your mother. She remembers it."

"But I'm asking you," I said. "When did you find out about the concentration camps? What was your reaction?"

"I didn't think about it. That was them and this was me," he said with a shrug.

Here was solipsism indeed: to ignore the greatest tragedy of modern times—of his own people!—because he wasn't personally involved. On the other hand, my father in his 80s is a hardly credible witness for the young man he was. What his reaction does underline is the pride he takes in being taciturn, and in refusing to cough up the conventionally pious response.

As I ask the Chinese waiter for the check, my father starts to fiddle with several napkins in his breast pocket. He has developed a curious relationship to these grubby paper napkins, which he keeps taking out of his pocket and checking. I've never seen him blow his nose with them. I wonder if old people have the equivalent of what clinical psychologists call "transitional objects"—like those pacifiers or teddy bears that children imbue with magical powers—and if these napkins are my father's talismen.

Just to show the internalized super-ego (God or my wife) that I have made an effort to *communicate*, I volunteer some news about myself. I tell my father that Cheryl and I are soon to have a baby. His response is: "*C'est la vie.*" This is carrying philosophic resignation too far—even good news is greeted stoically. I tell him we have bought a house, and my teaching post is secure. None of these items seems to register, much less impress. Either he doesn't get what I'm saying, or knows it already and is indifferent.

My older brother Hal called him recently with the news that he had had his first baby. On being told he was a grandfather, my father's answer was, "Federico Fellini just died." This became an instant family joke, along with his other memorable non sequiturs. (If indeed it was a non sequitur. The translation might be: "What do I care about your new baby when death is staring me in the face?") Though I could sympathize with Hal's viewing it as yet another dig to add to his copious brief against our father, who has always tend-ed to compete with his sons rather than rejoice in our good fortune, this Fellini response seemed to me more an expression of incapacity than insult. The frown on his face nowadays when you tell him something important, the *c'est la vie*, is a confession that he knows he can't focus enough to hold on to what you are saying; he lacks the adhesive cement of affect.

Even sports no longer matters to him. It used to be one of our few common topics: I was guaranteed a half-hour's worth of con-versation with my father, working my way through the Knicks, Mets, Rangers, Giants, Jets....His replies were curt, yet apt: "They stink. They got no hitting." He it was who taught me that passion-ate fandom that merges with disenchantment: loyalty to the local team, regardless of the stupid decisions the front office made; never cross a picket line, just stick with the union, for all their corruption; vote Democratic no matter how mediocre this year's slate. I would have thought being a sports fan was part of his invincible core, as much as his addiction to newspapers. He continues to have the Times ordered for him, but now it sits on his lap, unopened, like a ship passenger's blanket.

__Phillip Lopate__'s "The Story of My Father" has been excerpted from a longer essay of the same name. Lopate is the author of three essay collections, "Bachelorhood," "Against Joie de Vivre" and "Portrait of My Body." He also edited the anthology "The Art of the Personal Essay" and is currently editing an essay annual, to begin appearing in 1997. He is professor of English at Hofstra University.

Transit

K.E. Ellingson

I. Sic Kathryn: Monday Morning

*D*oing my usual Monday morning imitation of Lucifer descending, muttering sullen insurrection, I Kathryn, Archbitch of San Francisco (self-appointed), hurl myself into the abyss and thump perilously down the wet brick stairs into the BART station, mere seconds behind schedule. This particular feat ought to get me canonized, considering how late I rolled out of bed, groaning in despair, after having switched off the alarm and closing my heavyheavy eyelids for just one more minu ....

It was all Author's fault. OK, OK, a tiny bit my fault for letting him talk me into going out for a drink on Sunday night when I didn't really want to. At the Noe Valley Bar & Grill I was so bored and restless I ordered a second drink instead of insisting that Author take me home, and he was determined as usual to stay until closing, since his first class isn't until 9, which means he can get up as late as 8:30 if he doesn't shave, and he never shaves on Monday. I'm supposed to be *at* work at 8. What sadist thought that up, starting work at 8?

So I rushed around, threw clothes on, fed Catso, gulped a glass of refrigerator-flavored orange juice, gave my puffy gray face a lick and a promise instead of the thick mask of makeup it so desperately cried for, and managed to run out of the house only two minutes behind schedule. I could make up the two minutes in the six blocks to BART if I trotted along a little faster than my usual anaerobic, side-stitch pace, and if the lights were with me. *If.* But this was Monday morning and everything was against me, the whole physical world, probably the entire cosmos too if I only knew. Each light turned red as I approached, and the traffic surpassed ridiculous (where did all these aggressive assholes come from, is it a population

BUSINESS REPLY MAIL

FIRST CLASS MAIL   PERMIT NO. 17218-526   PITTSBURGH, PA

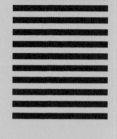

POSTAGE WILL BE PAID BY ADDRESSEE

CREATIVE NONFICTION
PO BOX 3000
DENVILLE NJ 07834-9259

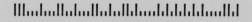

NO POSTAGE
NECESSARY
IF MAILED
IN THE
UNITED STATES

BUSINESS REPLY MAIL

FIRST CLASS MAIL   PERMIT NO. 17218-526   PITTSBURGH, PA

POSTAGE WILL BE PAID BY ADDRESSEE

CREATIVE NONFICTION
PO BOX 3000
DENVILLE NJ 07834-9259

explosion or what?); at the unmarked intersections, cars simply would not stop to let me cross. They could perhaps tell I was cross already. Once again I thought about going down to 15th and Guerrero and seeing if I couldn't get a deal on an automatic weapon. I could probably get my picture in the paper. "Woman Goes Berserk in Mission District Commute. Blames PMS." The six blocks to the 24th Street station had stretched to at least nine. It began to drizzle. No, actually, I hadn't brought my umbrella. Why would I have brought my umbrella, it's fucking *June*.

Near the bottom of the stairs I easily overtake a man handicapped by an overcoat and a fat briefcase. He's not bad looking, though a little too normal for my tastes, here however only an obstacle to be avoided. He stops to fumble for his ticket. I've got mine in my hand already, slip it into the slot as I bang through the turnstile ahead of him and run toward the escalator. I'm fast, but not quite fast enough to shove rudely in front of the two tubby chums who step together onto the same step, so that I can't get past; looming and glowering above them I descend slowly, no longer Lucifer but a statue (the Wingless Fury) settling oh so gradually into boggy ground. Halfway down I spy the 7:35's doors gliding closed. The dull silver train goes shooting away into the tunnel like... (I have been meditating on this image for the past few months) ...a chromed turd through a robot's intestine. How very passionately do I want to give these two simpering cows a hard push and send them sprawling. ("Moo, Moove!") Instead I say a little prayer: Why, God? Why do I have to dress up in these stupid clothes and mix with crowds? Why didn't I get my period, say, Friday, or even yesterday? I'll bet you my entire estate that it's going to be today, to help ensure that this week will be the worst in my life. Right, I mean the worst so far.

On the platform I commence pacing. It had to be the Concord train I just missed. Isn't it nice of them to have digital display clocks so you always know to the precise second how late your train is? It gives the harried commuter something to watch as the platform fills up and blood pressure soars. At 7:46 the 7:41 five-car Richmond train roars in (somebody's idea of a joke, running half a train at the height of the morning rush) and all 2,000 of us who have arrived in the last 12 minutes shuffle and jostle aboard. By now I am resigned. The die is cast at 7:44—if I haven't boarded a train by this time, no matter how fast I run, how agilely I dodge, how brazenly I jaywalk the six blocks from Montgomery Street station to the Pyramid, even if the elevator awaits me with open doors, I will be walking into the firm's tastefully decorated foyer at 8:03. And today being Monday ("Get Kathryn Day" in this part of the cosmos), I am willing to wager what's left of my estate that Mr. Big will be there in his specially made, voluminous gray suit with a dusting of dandruff on the shoulders, picking up the Wall Street Journal from my 6-foot by 5-foot rosewood desk, ready to give me a deeply reproachful look from his piggy little eyes. He's never *ever* there when I'm early.

The silver doors slide shut. I don't have the energy to move any further into the car (excuse me excuse me excuse me) which means when the train stops at 16th & Mission, the incoming crowd will crush me. Will crush me more. Deep in my spongy brain a migraine begins to throb; it feels like (I don't have to meditate on this image, it arises fully formed) a spike about the size of a tent peg hammered into the top of my skull until the tip is just behind my right eye. This is the unmistakable work of hormones (pronounced Whore-Moans and they didn't name them that for nothing). I also feel extremely hot. Someone nearby is wearing a lot of perfume, the one that smells just like Raid and always makes me marvel that anybody could put that on and think they smell good. Today, it makes me want to retch. Standing more or less in my armpit is a swarthy little man with the sad eyes of a spaniel, and I wonder how I smell, since I had no time for a morning shower. Well, too bad for him, that's what he gets for being so short.

I suppose it isn't rational that absolutely everything could be hopelessly impossible, but rational or not, so it all is, hopeless and impossible—writ large. I should have called in sick and stayed in bed—it was standing upright that assured the ruination of my day.

At the 16th & Mission station the train jerks to a stop, the doors open, and two people get off, giving me the opportunity to ooze past those clinging to the padded support posts (if they had straps to hang from they'd be strap-hangers; "post-clingers" doesn't, somehow, sing) and inch my way into the middle aisle, where I fight for a handhold on the top of the nearest seat. This is marginally better; I can stand here and loathe all the people seated. I cast my eyes along the rows. If only my misery loved company, then how my heart would rejoice, for everyone is looking bad this morning, and I don't think it's entirely an illusion caused by the color-leaching fluorescent lights. Even the exquisitely groomed, faultlessly turned out Filipinas from Daly City seem kind of peaked. My misery, however, does not love company. Anyway, if they all look almost as bad as I feel, I need only peer darkly into the windows as we enter the tunnel to confirm that I am feeling only as bad as I look: Monday morning, pea soup green. Lord Jesus Christ have mercy on my soul, I murmur to myself two or three times.

It doesn't help.

I try another formula: I wish I were dead. Seriously, I do. That would be better. Dead women don't commute.

Actually, an eternity of this cramped, vibrating misery under these cold lights would make a dandy prototype for hell. All of us damned, bilious and miserable, jammed into a black and gray tube, hurry-hurry-hurrying to what? To boring stupid work to make money to clothe and feed and sustain ourselves so we can keep working. I'm only in for three more months, and I suppose they all need the money to finance their habits, but what I don't understand is *how* they do it. Some people get up at 5 or 6 in the morning five days a week for years and years (I have even heard rumors of people who get up before 7 on weekends, but I don't believe everything I hear), and they don't go down to 15th & Guerrero and buy AK-16s and run amok, or not very often. What is their secret? Drugs? Positive thinking? I hate them, those lucky bastards. Even when I go to bed early, I can't wake up in the morning. If a doctor were to come and wake me up at 7 a.m. and evaluate my condition, he would grade it halfway between critical and guarded. (He would also remark on my abusive language.) And the worst part is, I'm in perfect health. I have the blood pressure of a child—not just any child but a hateful, disobedient one who won't shape up and face reality. I despise and abhor reality. I'll probably live to be 90, feeling like this.

As we pull into Civic Center, it occurs to me how simple it would be to get out, cross the platform and catch the next train back. I could be home in 15 minutes. Catso would be delighted to see me (not that he'd show it), and I could be back in bed before the clock struck 8:30 .... But no, I only have about three hours of sick leave, and I'm taking next Monday off (an eternity from now).

Besides, if wretchedness is my lot (and obviously it is), then I will drink it to the dregs, the bitterer the better. Me and my Unconquerable Soul. Anyway, bed wouldn't save me, there's no escape, it's everything that is awful. I need the damn money.

I must have thought the magic word, for right before my jaundiced eyes transpires a tiny miracle. The woman sitting immediately below me stands up to exit, and I have the next nearest standers blocked with my arm. I slither into the seat and find myself face to face with a young man in a well-cut black suit with a pinstripe. The suit and its pinstripe stink of craftmanship, quality, expense. The young man is as pinky clean as a freshly bathed and powdered baby; his hair is moussed, his nails manicured and buffed, even his mustache is styled and trimmed. I suspect that the soles of his glossy black shoes are clean. I want to kick dust all over him and set his mustache on fire.

My dislike is so vehement that it gives me a perverse delight to sit, staring insolently at him. I know his sort—a positive thinker. If I asked him, he'd boast complacently that he only needs four hours of sleep a night and he loves his job (only he'd refer to it as "my position.") He's second in command somewhere, not Mr. Big, not yet, but Mr. Ambitious Young Man on the Way Up. One of those know-it-all turkeys who practices being aggressive and rude on the phone, while in person he simpers and preens. I deal with them daily. I like to say, "Is he expecting you?" in a fuck-you tone, and then direct them to chairs and watch them slowly deflate until such time as someone comes to fetch them. I've been at the Partnership three months, and I need to stick it out at least three more. It's not a bad job, as jobs go, but I'm fed up with playing my role, and bored with trying to cajole a human response out of those self-important popinjays. The only people who show any good manners are the "sales reps" whose affirmations in the face of constant rejection precede them like a whiff of discreet but still offensive cologne. They aren't supposed to be up hustling sales in the penthouse suites, but if they walk by the guards without hesitating, they can hustle freely until they are reported and escorted out. I turn them all away but only after volunteering to pass along their business cards to the office manager who never does much of anything besides collect business cards and make personal phone calls. The only people I unreservedly like are the delivery people, Fed Ex and UPS, as well as the sweaty bike messengers; they all have the air of nonconformist and outlaw about them.

Mr. Ambitious looks up at me from his WSJ but I don't drop my eyes or react, and he quickly turns his glance away to the window. Ha ha, stared you down, I silently gloat, wishing I'd worn my snake wig. The train barrels into the Powell Street station and slams to a halt, as if the driver just woke from his nap in the nick of time. I am catapulted forward, halfway out of my seat, but brace my feet and plop back again. The woman sitting next to me says, "Geez," and I almost smile, because I was so nearly launched head first into Mr. Ambitious' black gabardine, pin-striped lap, as if diving for treasure. That would have surprised him, I think smugly. Mr. Ambitious, misinterpreting my smirk, smiles back at me. Oh, no you don't—I instantly clear my expression to impassive and turn to examine the people across the aisle.

I look up the car and then down. It's too much for my frayed wiring. In all my years of commuting, I have never seen such a ... Maybe I am going mad. Just like this on a BART train. I've sometimes wondered just how it would announce itself ... how else but with everybody turning into cartoons. I've gotten trapped in the dominion of caricature. Many of my fellow passengers appear to be illustrations of vices, while some could be Brueghel peasants, vacant with imbecility yet cunning and malicious; not a few resemble animals—there are a few sheep, a boar, a weasel, many dogs, even more monkeys, but no cats this morning, no moles. Just across the aisle from me, a woman with duck lips sits next to Elmer Fudd; facing them a knave and a fool, and beyond a receding series of freaks, sociopaths and mutations. Down yonder I spy Einstein, Hitler, Geraldo and Liz. And here am I: Caliban, Thersites and Timon of Athens all rolled into one. A big green, spleeny one.

The world is so lucky that I don't have nuclear weapons on Monday mornings. More than anything I want to stand up and shout, "You loathsome vermin, get off my planet!"

I do stand up, but merely because we are approaching the Montgomery Street station. This day will never end and I will never feel better but I don't care because feeling better is a lie anyway. There's nothing to be done but to get on with it. Geronimo! I am first up at the door that will end up nearest the escalators. Just as we coast to a stop an East Bay train comes to rest across the platform. All the doors open simultaneously: Happy Monday and chaos come again! I dash out in the clear for two seconds, then have to dodge to sidestep a tiny woman mincing along in a tight skirt and spike heels. I want to bellow like a moose, but clench my teeth around "Move it" and keep going. Someday somebody's going to get killed in here and golly, I hope it's me. The escalator is already a bottleneck. No way there. With a color movie of random violence—a comedy—playing in my brain, I sprint for the stairs and take the steps two at a time.

II. Kathryn in Excelsis: Friday Afternoon

I'm waiting for the elevator at 4:30 when Danny comes running out with a bulging manila envelope. "Hold that elevator," he commands in his executive voice. "I've got to deliver these important documents ASAP. Fox, Rat, Badger & Big are counting on me!" We leave together; I can't tell what's making my stomach go like that, the elevator's descent or 21-year-old, green-eyed Danny who in three days has won my heart. He says, "If any of *them* get in with us, let's stick our tongues out at them." "Good idea," I say, prepared to agree with anything Danny suggests, and when the young couple in suits, carrying briefcases and talking enthusiastically about bonds and securities, gets in at the 24th floor, we both extrude our tongues the merest quarter inch and ride down to the plaza level gazing at the couple like cats. The man, pompously blabbing, doesn't notice, but the woman watches us with a nervous little smile.

See how in a few tomorrows everything has changed: I love the whole damn beautiful world, I do, but I especially love San Francisco and if perhaps not quite all the people in it, most of them. OK, many of them. And even the worst have their, shall we say, perverse charm. Today I'm even rather amused by the Yuppies doing their Yuppie thing, blocking the sidewalk, chatting with fatuous self-assurance, clogging the streets with their BMWs and Volvos, playing their car stereos or yakking on their cellular phones while the air outside fills with sulphurous fumes. I mean I enjoy the spectacle, the bustle. The wind is blowing the fumes over to Oakland anyway. Sorry, Oakland.

Our elevator alights in the lobby of the pyramid, which proves to be thronged with people waiting, I can tell, for their lovers. Not a few of them hold bouquets of flowers in paper or plastic cones, which pleases me as much as if they had all been bought for me. Danny pushes open the door, saying "Allow me" in a comically gallant voice. Outside, the summer afternoon presents revels of sound and light: A brisk breeze snaps the gaudy pennants above the plaza, and the sun chips diamonds off the laughing spray of the fountain. Pigeons dance the pigeon strut beneath redwood benches to the trumpet call of gridlocked traffic echoing from the architectonic canyons of California Street. Danny tells me a long story about some amazing adventure that happened to him and his brother last weekend, lingering a moment at his turn-off and touching my arm before saying goodbye. Light-headed from hyperventilation brought on by an acute outbreak of lust, I begin to waltz down Sacramento Street toward the Embarcadero station, knowing full well what the future holds and not minding that it is sure to end badly; sometimes when you see disaster looming, you have to run to embrace it. I will, yes ... but not today. Today my goals are more modest: I'm going to get a seat for the ride home or spit.

It couldn't be any afternoon but Friday. Half the crowd on the sidewalk strides along purposefully while the other half saunters, yet there are no collisions and all appear pleased with whatever pace they keep. At Sacramento and Front I heel up behind a troop of Japanese businessmen all in identical dark suits and identical striped ties, with identical cameras hanging around their necks, all staring in apparently identical fascination at the more motley Californian office people pouring forth from the high-rises. Perhaps because the tallest of them is just my height, they remind me of a strange bunch of Boy Scouts. They pivot as one to gawk at a Junoesque black woman arrayed in flowing white robes and a feathered turban, sailing down the middle of the sidewalk like a galleon before the wind and parting the crowd with her imposing prow. Two runners in skimpy outfits of crimson and gold nylon cross her wake at right angles, leap in unison and speed away. A rotund, bald man wearing a ring on each finger and—can it be?—a diamond choker stoops to pick up the quivering little terrier that the nimble-jack runners had hopped.

"Poopsie, are you all right?" he cries dramatically, and Poopsie, who also wears a diamond choker, licks his face.

Of course Poopsie all right. Everything is all right. Humming the "Ode to Joy:" *Freu-de, freu-de,* I gather it, every last bit I can reach, as it whirls around me. Festival, procession, pageant. I am so buoyant I rebound from the pavement with each step as if concrete were rubber, *pour mieux sauter.* Down the road I skip, step-sauté, step-sauté in time to the "Ode." At the corner of Davis Street, waiting for the light to change, I glance around and behold: There he stands in front of the Embarcadero, the god Frey himself incarnate as a black haired youth (about Danny's age), radiant in tennis whites, carrying a squash racket, dancing in the late afternoon sun. He must have a great tape in his Walkman, because he's playing air guitar on his squash racket and working it out like some orgiastic rock & roller, say, Jimmy Page in his heyday. His revel takes place in complete silence, and if anybody wants to stare, my pagan lord is too far gone in pleasure to care. Amazingly, no one passing by so much as turns his head; probably Frey is only visible to the faithful. My mouth opens, and I have to raise my hand to contain the sugary ooze of my smile. How I want to run over and give him a kiss, just one (to start with) … but the light changes to green, the next thing summons me, and I must go.

I switch my song to a devilish old blues numbah and actually sing out loud (but softly, I'm not crazy yet), and in the ambient enchantment am transformed into a blues ballerina, all hips and breasts, in funky gossamer white chiffon with a shimmy of seed pearls. Wearing Friday's freedom-*freuden* as my tiara of flame, I do the do the rest of the way to BART, and light as a snowflake and sweeter than jelly roll, float down the stairs into the station, singing deep in my throat. The overhead signs start flashing the approach of my train as I pirouette onto the platform

K.E. Ellingson *prefers reading to writing and only writes because she secretly believes that if she doesn't, her head will fill up with words until it explodes. She currently resides in Seattle and dreams of elsewhere.*

At the Buzzer

Michael Berberich

A while back, for the first and only time in my
life, I hit six free throws in a row. I was alone on my side of the
court, so I looked around to see if anyone had taken notice of this,
the pinnacle of my basketball life. I longed to hear the crowd going
wild. At the other end of the court a couple of kids in their teens
took shots from around the perimeter with a third fellow, a stocky
guy in his mid-20s decked in a sweat suit emblazoned with the official seal of the University of Minnesota. The younger teen, sporting
a smudged Knicks jersey, appeared to be about 16. He and I were
about the same size and build, a lanky 5 feet 10 inches. His 18- or
19-year-old pal, a bean pole draped in an oversized T-shirt with the
words "Shaq Attack" on it, had a good two or three inches over the
rest of us. The threesome shared two very well-worn basketballs.

"You wanna run?" the Shaq-man called out. Street talk has
changed since my day. It sounded like a sincere question, lacking any
threatening tone to suggest he was telling me to scram. It sounded
almost like he was asking me if I wanted to play.

I am 38 years old. I have a slight paunch, which is why I started
going to the solitary basketball court in the park next to the yacht
basin around the corner from my apartment. I live but a few short
blocks away from the Gulf of Mexico. I imagined pleasant afternoons shooting hoops by myself, perhaps in the presence of the
slightest of breezes, the traces of salt and seaweed borne lightly to
cool and soothe me in repayment for my exertions.

I have my routine: I bend and stretch on the lawn next to the
court for 10 minutes or so; then I try layups for another 10 or 15

minutes. Lastly, loose and limber, I shoot exactly 100 free throws before calling it quits.

I love shooting free throws. Shooting free throws is one of the few activities that allow at one and the same time intense concentration and a full play of the imagination. I imagine it must have been basketball that gave us that wonderful all-encompassing metaphor "on the line" as in "with one second left and his team down by a point, Berberich steps up to the line to shoot one and one. Holy moly, the championship is on the line, folks!" Concentration and imagination, that's all it takes, concentration and imagination. A bloke can get away with saying things like that on the day he nails six free throws in a row.

If I get off to a late start I am sometimes chased off the court by young teens just getting out of school. As for the three guys at the other end of the court, Shaq-man and Minnesota Man were old enough not to be in school if they didn't want to be. I decided that the Knickerbocker Kid, however, must be playing hooky. Either that or he dropped out of school so he could play basketball all day long. There have been days I would have liked to do the same.

To tell the truth, I am never actually run off the court by pubescent Charles Barkley wannabes. I know that I do not belong on the court with boys. I am not one of them. We play for different reasons. They play because, in a sense, they have to. Mother Nature has them running on high octane, whereas I run on regular unleaded. I just want to drop a few pounds and keep the ol' heart thumping at an accelerated pace for an hour or so three or four times a week to keep the doctor from giving me a hard time during my annual checkup. Still, I wondered, should I run with them?

I didn't recognize any of these guys. On those days when the neighborhood crew shows up after school but before I have finished my hundred free throws, I simply take shots from the corner, not leaving until I sink one from 15 feet or so. Who knows, I could be run over by a bus or struck by lightning before my next workout on the courts. I would not want to die knowing I had missed the last shot at the buzzer. There are times when you get to write your own rules, and since such times come few and far between in real life, my rule is that no one runs me off the court 'til I sink a game winner from the corner. Mission accomplished, I depart—usually grumbling something about kids not having enough homework these days. Never before had I been invited to play.

On those occasions when I completed my hundred free throws, my best performance came on a glorious, windless, sun-drenched afternoon when I knocked down a deadly 35 percent. I was so excited I went straight home and even before showering pored over the paper to see where I would rank in the NBA if, say, I had made my 35 of 100 free throws while playing for the Houston Rockets. Of course, Hakeem's got nothing to worry about, but maybe down at the bottom of the statistics there was some benchwarming lunk I could boast I was better than.

So on the day when I made six free throws in a row, this young man asked me if I wanted to "run." I hadn't played in a street game in 20 years, at least.

"I'm just an old, out-of-shape guy," I proffered. "I'm no good." If that charming piece of fluff, "White Men Can't Jump," was good for nothing else, it at least made studs on the street look upon such claims as mine with a modicum of skepticism.

Shaq-man said, "We need four. We can't run with three."

I hesitated. Sensing my reluctance, the Knickerbocker Kid blurted out, "I seen you shoot."

That did it: I, the guy always picked last on any team, the guy who the high school P.E. coach once called "Meat"—the wit of which was not lost on the rest of the class who cracked up laughing and called me Meat for the rest of the year; I who had never lettered in any sport in my life, who had once been stood up on a date by the prettiest girl in the school only to discover, when I went to the movie alone, that my dream girl had slipped into the movie just after the lights dimmed and sat through the movie in the back row making out with the catcher on the baseball team, a lummox whose fingers had the shape of cucumbers and whose greatest intellectual achievement was that he invented the classroom entertainment of taking a pea shooter and shooting spit wads at the blackboard to see if he could dot the "i" before the teacher could.

The teacher in that class, Ms. Effie Griswold, was an aged and infirm but kindly dowager, so it was never quite certain who would win the race to dot the chalked "i." In fact, once after she dropped her chalk on the floor and stooped to pick it up we held a contest, with the whole class shooting little white flecks of chewed paper to see who could come closest to dotting the "i." By the time Ms. Griswold got back about the business of dotting the "i," the blackboard looked like a map of the Milky Way with an entire galaxy of spit wads clustered around the "i" in a great, looping swirl that would have made Carl Sagan proud. Looking at the bespeckled board, Ms. Griswold stopped suddenly and turned slowly toward the class. Then she set the chalk down, removed her glasses, took out a handkerchief and commenced wiping her lenses. Turning back to face the board, she paused, started to set the chalk down again, stopped, sighed, and at last, with an almost palsied hand, set about completing the sentence on the board. At any rate, I was no good at that sport either.

You understand, then, just how susceptible I was to the flattering faux pas by the Knickerbocker Kid. I had made six free throws in a row and, to top it off, someone in the world had noticed! Surely this was my day. How could I refuse to run? How could life get any better?

"So how do we choose up?" I asked, long out of touch with street etiquette.

"First two," Shaq-man replied, bouncing a worn pee-wee-sized ball twice before canning a perfect shot which dropped through the broken chain net with a nice ka-chink sound. I stepped up to the line, balanced the ball in my hands, twirled and bounced it once, raised it, cocked, released, followed through, and watched the ball hit the left side of the rim, rattle around inside the hoop a couple of times, and fall to the side, thus ending my streak. The shot was close enough that I had saved face, however. "Bad luck," the Knickerbocker Kid said. He still thought I could shoot. Some things truly are eternal, and I remained thankful for one of those verities—that young men are tenaciously unwilling to give up their illusions.

Minnesota Man, the mid-20ish fellow, uncorked a shot from the top of the key. His was a smooth, fluid shot, and though his shot hit the front of the steel and caromed right back to his hands, clearly he had a natural touch. The Knickerbocker Kid, my deluded admirer, quickly knocked down a jumper, and the teams were set: It would be the young guns versus the old bums. Heck, I was easily at least 10 years older than anyone else on the court; I pondered, Was this what it felt like for Kareem in his dotage? Would my very first game in the big time also be my farewell tour?

The match-ups needed no discussion. I stacked up well against the Knickerbocker Kid, if for no other reason than he was still under the illusion that I could shoot. I wondered how long I could keep him fooled. Minnesota Man would guard Shaq-man, mostly because he had far greater upper body strength than I, undoubtedly developed by many long winters of shoveling snow.

"Which ball?" I asked, utterly convinced they would choose mine. It was by far the newest ball, and it was the only one that was properly inflated.

Shaq-man quickly discarded the pee-wee ball. My new teammate, Minnesota Man, took my ball and unleashed a perfect swisher from his favorite spot at the top of the key. "It feels a little slippery, but it'll do," he said.

The Knickerbocker Kid passed my ball back out to Shaq-man who, without a dribble, lofted a 12-footer that swirled around the hole before spinning out. "I like this one better," he said, picking up the velvety soft but somewhat underinflated third ball that the threesome had shared while shooting around.

"Suit yourself," said Minnesota Man. I felt a twinge. My perfectly good ball had been rejected in favor of a ball that had about as much appeal as a wilted head of cabbage. Of course, I took it personally—who wouldn't?—but being the new kid on the block, so to speak, I said nothing.

To start the game, I inned the ball to Minnesota Man who, covered by the Shaq-man, swept around to the right corner and then snapped a pass back to me, darting straight toward the hoop from half court with the Knickerbocker Kid trailing from my backside. He was beat. There was a problem, though. I had to slow my charge to the net just a tad to compensate for the damn slow bounce of this wimpy ball. Shaq-man spun away from his man and scrambled to cut off my drive. I dished the ball back to Minnesota Man who set himself and knocked down the bucket to give us the first score and a 1-0 lead.

For the next few minutes we learned about one another, cutting in and out, pushing and shoving, twisting, turning and taunting. "Man, you older than Moses!" the Knickerbocker Kid whined goodnaturedly. I've certainly had worse said of me. I set the record straight, informing him that I taught Malone everything he knows.

The Shaq-man had quick hands and could connect from any- where on the court. The Knickerbocker Kid preferred to shoot from the left side of the court. My earlier impression about Minnesota Man's nice touch proved true. And with some sharp passing, I tried to delay the discovery that, as a basketball player, I was an imposter. My greatest asset was self-knowledge: I knew I was lousy, my six free throws in a row notwithstanding.

Within minutes, Minnesota Man and I were down 5-3. One of our points came when I made an easy layup, this time because Shaq- man stayed on his man, leaving me an easy garbage shot.

Already feeling winded, I suddenly found myself guarding the Shaq-man one on one. In the backcourt we crouched face to face. Suddenly he took a quick step to my left. I expected him to blow right by me. But in that instant I discovered something crucial: Shaq- man, too, had to slow down to wait for the ball to bounce back up. I reached in and tapped the ball out of bounds. What a sucker! He'd been set up and duped by Minnesota Man. My teammate had com- mented on the slipperiness of my relatively new ball but said it would do, and the Shaq-man, fearing some slight advantage in our favor, had insisted on a ball that took away his quickness. Indeed, I thought, old age and treachery do overcome youth and inexperi- ence. No longer worried about being unable to keep up with my man, I commenced making a pest of myself on defense.

Something else became readily apparent. Neither the Shaq-man nor the Knickerbocker Kid much liked to pass the ball. If we dou- ble-teamed the Kid, half the time he'd toss up a brick and then mut- ter "Sheeyit!" when the shot missed. Collapsing our defense to double-team the Shaq-man when he got close to the bucket posed a different problem. Shaq-man liked to take the ball to the hole whether he had a shot or not. If his shot was off, with his height and vertical leap he stood a better chance of grabbing the offensive board and slamming home the follow-up shot.

Via craftiness and duplicity, we caught up with the young guns, tying the score at 8. A minute later, I deflected a shot by the Knickerbocker Kid, Minnesota Man snagged the loose ball, juked

Shaq-man off his feet by feigning a jumper, and then scooted underneath for an uncontested layup.

We could not hold the lead. The Knickerbocker Kid quickly dropped a shot of such exquisite beauty that the chains seemed untrifled as the ball slipped through with nary a whisper. The shot was of such perfection even the Shaq-man smiled.

After another exchange of points, at just about the time the Kid had me figured out for the poseur that I was, I pulled up for a shot but had to hold back when the Knickerbocker Kid engulfed me with a smothering defense. His arms waved up and down, back and forth, and his hands reached out, almost stripping the ball from me at one point. When no outlet pass developed, I unfurled a 10-foot hook shot. The chains rattled, the Kid shook his head, and once again my team had a one point lead. He seen me shoot, all right! I think I had hit a shot like that once back in the sixth grade but certainly hadn't hit one since then. It's easy enough to remember such moments of glory when they only happen once every 20 years. And on a day when you hit six free throws in a row, what's the harm in trying a rusty hook shot as well?

With us holding an edge 13-12 and me mismatched against the Shaq-man, the Knickerbocker Kid whipped a sharp cross-court pass, and before I knew it the Shaq-man was airborne. I had but a split second to make my decision. With complete abandon and selflessness I could throw my body in Shaq-man's way, take the charge, block the shot, and hope my family spent the payoff on my life insurance wisely, or I could slide halfway out of the way and duck. I ducked. I held onto my glasses, all the better with which to see the two shoes, toes pointed downward, which floated by six inches from my face. I could smell leather. The Shaq-man rammed the ball through the steel, held onto the quivering rim with both hands, and released a primal scream. I cowered.

There was no hiding the fact any longer. As it always does, the truth reared its ugly visage. I stood exposed. I really was no good.

Minnesota Man inned the ball to me, and I swept around to the left corner. His right hand reaching toward my face, the Knickerbocker Kid stayed between me and the basket. Shaq-man and Minnesota Man jostled each other for position just to the right of the basket. Carefully guarding the ball, bouncing it low to the ground and away from my body, I shouldered my way toward center court. I stopped right at the free-throw line. Suddenly Minnesota Man cut from the front side of the court and streaked back toward the top of the key. I froze the Knickerbocker Kid by eyeing the basket and then flipped the ball blind behind my back, a perfect shuffle to my partner who swept around to my left, leaving Shaq-man in his wake. Pulling up, he banked an easy jumper. At 14-13, we were one point away from victory.

The Kid got the in-bounds pass to the Shaq-man. Hoping for a pass on a fast break, the Kid broke straight for the net but, stepping in front of him, I refused to budge. Like so many of his unruly counterparts these days, he had lost all respect for his elders. He tried forcing his way through me to the hoop. Our shoulders bumped, our arms entangled, and then I shoved him away to the outside. No matter. Shaq-man had no intention of passing the ball. Pivoting left, then spinning right, Shaq-man launched his shot from 12 feet. The ball curled from the right to the left of the rim, whipping out on my side. I had position, went up, brought down the rebound with both hands, and then flared my elbows, swinging them back and forth in my best Bill Laimbeer imitation. If we scored now the game would be ours.

With the Knickerbocker Kid between me and the hoop, I had no shot. I cleared the key. Minnesota Man wandered backcourt, waiting open for the ball. Shaq-man played him loose, giving him the open half-court shot. I considered using my hook shot again. After all, if I could hit six free throws in a row, why not go for back-to-back sky hooks? The Knickerbocker Kid pressed his left hand against my chest, his right hand waving in blocking position. His eyes darted back and forth between me and Minnesota Man. The Kid wasn't worried about me in the least. Obviously, neither was the Shaq-man.

Minnesota Man moved all the way to the back line. Clearly the Shaq-man was willing to gamble against him taking and making a half-court shot. Should the shot miss, the rebound would assuredly go to the Shaq-man, who'd have an easy slam to tie the game. I dished the ball cleanly back to Minnesota Man, who took a couple of steps up and before the Shaq-man could get there unloaded a 24-foot bomb. Ka-chink. Nuthin' but net!

We exchanged quick pleasantries and then almost immediately dispersed. The Knickerbocker Kid scooped his pee-wee ball from the lawn behind the pole, and then he and Shaq-man headed off, laughing and joking. I wondered about the kind of life that an out-of-school 16-year-old returns to. Minnesota Man meandered towards the yacht basin, every once in a while tossing his underinflated ball from one hand to the other. I stuck around for a few moments, first to catch my breath, then to sink my obligatory corner shot at the buzzer before leaving.

Post Script: I am no longer able to shoot free throws or "run" in pickup games. The City's Parks and Recreations Department shut down the basketball court in the park by the yacht club. Basketball courts are nice things to have in upscale neighborhoods so long as nobody ever really uses them. Or so long as only the "right" people use them.

The Parks and Rec secretary I spoke with claimed that Galveston was just following a "national trend" in the closing of outdoor public basketball courts. In middle-class neighborhoods, that is. The stated reason for the closing of the courts was that they had become "havens for drug dealing and gathering places for young criminals." Closing the courts was the "only" answer these imaginative bureaucrats could devise. The unstated reason for the closing of the courts, of course, is that they drew black youths into middle-class, largely white neighborhoods.

The irony is that the courts were shut down because they did exactly what they were supposed to do: They extended the "boundaries" of the neighborhood, drawing together people who would not otherwise be part of the same community. And that, it seems, is still a problem in America today.

Michael Berberich *has had several essays about gambling and public policy published in Notre Dame Magazine and has had an essay about baseball published by the National Endowment for the Humanities.*

Radio Wars, Closed Doors, When You're Out I Check Your Drawers

Elizabeth Hodges

*I*t's 1964. In her room my sister turns her radio up high. Eighteen and a half, her door shut tight. Scratchy voices croon shriek yodel about love. I have peeked through the space around her door's latch and seen her dancing like some tribeswoman out of National Geographic, the brown, plastic, radio icon urging her on from its place atop her highboy. I can imagine her in there now, undulating in the tension of radio static and the tension of the time she has yet to wait before her date comes and carries her off in his car, its radio, same station, same static, same scratchy voices wheedling weeping wailing about love. Songs' lyrics blur. All are war cries to my classical soul, abrasions to my ear drums. I am 11 in 33 days and nine hours. I am a classical pianist, seven and a half years of study stored in my long muscular fingers. For five of those years, I have been working with a retired concert pianist and teacher from the Peabody Institute of Music. I am good, and I see no reason for anything more contemporary than Gershwin, Rodgers and Hammerstein, Lerner and Loewe—those great writers of great musicals. And of course I embrace the melodious Nelson Eddy and Jeanette MacDonald. My mother loves to sing with them, and I do, too. "When I'm calling you-oo-oo-oo—oo-oo-oo." My sister sings, but I never hear her do so outside of church choir; there, I can always hear her voice, separate from the 25 singers. Her voice is true and strong. She can bring a hymn to life. But outside of church, her taste in music stinks.

From her room, behind her tightly closed door, a Beatles' song begins. Behind my door, also closed tight, I turn my radio on and crank it high. Static pricks the air in my room as in hers, but at least amid my static sing woodwinds and French horns, violins and violas, cohesive in a rich frenzy, heart-palpitating anger trading remarks with abrupt softenings, soothing calms. Mozart's Symphony No. 40. In G minor. Two flats. B and E. My sister's radio takes up my challenge. Some guy whining out of tune and through his nose, "How many roads must a man walk down, before you can call him a man?" *A few more than you,* I smirk. I raise Mozart to new heights. My sister cranks her radio, too. I crank once again, top volume. She cranks again, and I am disarmed. She has more power. The frenzy of Mozart's first movement ends as he gives in to "I wanna hold your hand." I give in too, turn my radio off, and throw my door open to glare in fury at hers. Psychic, she opens her door to give me that smile, that slightly sweet, slightly crooked curve of closed lips that always makes me feel short and misunderstood, trapped in my child body. I am nearly angry enough to yell, to lunge. But the moment is defused. Astute and always punctual, my mother calls up the stairs with what is the eternal question for my sister and me, "Is anything wrong up there?" What can we do but bond and assure her? "Oh, no!" she responds. "Nothing!" I add. "Just playing around!" she adds, calling cheerfully. I pinch my face into the worst grimace I can imagine and point it at her. "Just seeing whose radio is louder," my sister adds, grins and gloats. We *know* whose radio is louder. Mom retreats, knowing that, of course, something is wrong, but not what, and how could either of us explain anyway.

What would my sister say if she answered honestly? *Betsy is a brat? I hate having her in my space?* (The whole second floor of our small house truly was her whole space until I was 8.) *She leaves the bathroom a mess? She messes with my make-up and ruins the Noxzema?* Guilty as charged. Guilty as charged. I make messes and don't see them until someone else does. I ruined her mascara, but accidentally. And it left telltale smudges and streaks that I didn't see. And the Noxzema, I use it. I wash my face with it. Mom buys it. I don't want blackheads and pimples to grow because my grandmother loves to go after them. I have watched her corner my older cousins and check their ears and fidget around their noses. Sharp nails. She loves teenage backs the best. So I use the Noxzema just like it says to on its label. But, last week, I left the lid off, and the white cream yellowed and developed a thick skin, pulling away from the side of the jar. My sister said it was done for, didn't even put the lid on it, just left it on the back of the toilet where I left it. Now it is beyond rehydrating, a shrunken, hard marshmallow stuck in cobalt-blue glass. It has become crisscrossed with fissures like the parched, arid regions in the National Geographic.

Could she tell Mom, *I don't trust her to stay out of my room when I'm out?* And there is absolutely no reason she should trust me. I have graduated from sticking to the narrow confines of that invisible trail she demarcated several years before, from her door to my office. I am now up to opening and looking—any box, any drawer, her closet. I have not progressed to touching and lifting, and might not. But looking and studying the artifacts of my sister has become serious work, the work of the solver of mysteries, the work of the anthropologist. Who is this young woman with the dark chocolate hair? What does she think? Want? Love? Is she afraid of anything? It never seems so anymore. Does she know her future? Does she love this boyfriend? Does she kiss him? Does he write her love letters? Where would she keep them? The mattress.

This is much more than nosiness. I need to know her, and I hunt her down amongst her possessions, but I haven't found her yet. I find parts—a silver filigree friendship ring, a sand dollar from our trip to Florida.

The best part of that trip was when we drove out to Captiva Island and across the sandbar to Sanibel Island. My piano teacher, with whom I share a passion for finding shells, told us about these islands. So we went, and there on Sanibel was a resort under construction, not necessarily open for business, but happy for visitors when they showed up. We stayed five days, a week perhaps, in a two-room cottage for $25 a night. The restaurant was open and the food clearly gourmet, even to my neophyte palate. That's what the chef said. "You haf a ney-o-feet pal-laht, mademoiselle, but clear a good pal-laht. I will train eet some, *n'est-ce pas?*" And he did. He did. My sister got a crush on the waiter, Ed, red hair, zits. He took us into the jungle part of the island, birding. Anhingas. Wood storks. And ivory-billed woodpeckers, not the pileated we often see in Catoctin. Ivory-billed, not extinct yet after all. He took us shelling. We waded, me chest deep, feeling with our bare feet for sand dollars, He and my sister held hands. I was in the way, inevitable, invaluable. They couldn't leave our temporary home without me. So they held hands and probably nothing more, no kissing, and at times, for fun, I pushed against the limits of my value on the Gulf side of the island, where we'd walk to look for sharks, me following 8 feet or so behind, puckering my lips and making kissy sounds. And singing their joy sweetly. "My sister has a boyfriend."

The strait between the islands and the west coast of Florida was crystal clear like an aquamarine and protected against sharks by dolphins. White pelicans sat everywhere. When we left, I brought back 25 sand dollars, several conchs and some other shells—all priceless to me, all alive until Ed helped me commit molluskicide and store the sand dollars and shells in Clorox and water in the trunk of our car. All the way back to Maryland the scent of dead mollusks grew greater and seeped around the invisible gaps between trunk and passenger compartment into the back seat. The smell was horrendous, sickening, but the shells made it home and into my collection.

I wonder if she keeps the sand dollar to remember Ed. I wonder who gave her the silver ring. I wonder and wonder, but I can never put the pieces together. She is the puzzle I may never solve. And I feel time getting close because she is almost an adult. She might move out too soon, but not for her. She knows me. She is right. When she leaves for her date tonight, I am going to explore one or two of the narrow shelves in her closet, and I am going to lift her mattress to check for love letters. And if I find any, I might just read them. I am also thinking about unplugging her radio.

So what would I answer if I answered my mother honestly when she asked if there was anything wrong up here? *There are too many rules up here, Mom? Why can't I read for a while before I go to bed?* Reading under covers with a flashlight is not all it's cracked up to be. Bach went blind partly because he spent his childhood nights penning masterpieces in secret by the light of the moon. *Why can't I have my radio on low when I go to sleep? Why can't I turn on my light when I have a nightmare or when I simply can't sleep?* Why does she always promise to tell? And why don't I let her? What would have happened if she did tell? And would she ever really tell?

But most important, I would ask Mom, *Why am I only a pest? I am a pest, it's true. But I wouldn't be if I didn't have to be. Do you understand? I have to be a pest. I am too young to be a friend.*

As Mom retreats, no doubt to confer with Dad, we, too, retreat to our rooms and our secret identities as tormentors and tormented. She turns her radio up, just some. I leave mine off.

Through the wall between our rooms, I can hear the Beatles again. Stupid stupid stupid music. I hate the Beatles, partly because their music does not, for me, qualify as music, but more because they drive girls, even girls my age, googah. Everybody loves them. Every girl in the fifth grade has picked out which Beatle she's going to marry. When people go to Beatles concerts, they stand on their seats and scream so loud that they cannot even hear the music they paid to hear. So they didn't go to hear the music. It seems like the Beatles get paid just to come out in front of an audience to get screamed at. In some way or another, the Beatles surround me all day and all night.

But not this evening. With two of my sister's cotton balls soaked in warm water and wrung out, I shut my door and wedge myself into the right corner at the head of my bed, the furthest point in my room from the wall that separates her from me. I stuff the cotton balls into my ears and pull one of the books from beneath my pillow. I try to lose myself and my fury in the trials and tribulations of "The Middle Sister," a girl from the pioneer days, true, but her story is the same as mine, except that she gets a chance to do something so brave that she is never just the middle sister again. She makes an apple tart for an Indian who comes into the house while her family is in town and she is supposed to be cleaning and making dinner for their return. Her fear is split between the Indian and what her mother and father will do about her using the last of the stored apples to make him the pacifying tart. He eats and is peaceful when her family returns. She is a heroine. Her joy fills her chest and mine. I pull out the cotton and re-enter my world and hear silence. My sister has gone out. I tiptoe to my door, open and confirm. Her door hangs open on its black iron, pseudo-colonial hinges, and her light is off. I take up my flashlight and begin the search.

There are some wars between people which start in the gut and bypass reason. My sister and I had those wars a lot. She knew just how to push me into action against myself. I knew how to get her riled. Our wars, like all wars, were about territory and power. Like all wars, they began with a slightly faster rush of blood in the veins in response to some almost imperceptible movement. Then a nudge from one side, a pushing back from the other, a shove, a harder shove and—escalation, elevation—the rocketing, spiralling, out-of-control, full-scale war, both sides giving as much as they could to give as good as they got. Unlike most warriors, my sister and I left no gaping wounds or scars. Skirmishes were guerrilla, often silent and devastating, quick as the strike of a snake. Retreats were strategic and as fast as a moray drawing back into his crevice, only to strike again. Take the war of the closed bedroom doors, for example. I don't know why this single event sticks with me, but it has, perhaps because it was a true matching of wits, and she won.

Our bedroom doors were knotty pine, not with knobs, but with latches like some garden gates have—on the inside, a flat bar which is lifted and let down by a metal lever that goes through a hole below the bar, outer door to inner door. When the door was closed, the bar crossed the crack between door and jamb and fell behind a metal catch on the jamb. The doors would close, but they would not lock. Thus neither of us was secure from interruption, invasion, and the space around the lever encouraged spying. There was one day, though, when the issue of locking surfaced big time, just that once and never again. I cannot remember who started it. I remember that it started as a game of sorts, fun, then lessening fun, then fervor, then fury. I can only start after the game had begun.

If the lever won't move, the bar can't lift. So I stuff small wads of paper into the space around the lever. I test it. It cannot move. I go sit on my bed and watch as my sister pokes the paper out with a No. 4 pencil. She snaps the lever up, and *ta-da!*, she has my door open. She waltzes back to her room. I try again. *If the lever won't move, the bar won't lift.*

So I fold paper until it is thick enough to force down between the bar and the door. *If the bar is too tight, the lever won't move.* I step back and wait, longer this time. I feel her studying the problem. I hear a grunt of satisfaction. A minute later, I watch as the thin, steel blade of her painting spatula slides in and down the crack between the door and jamb and shoves my thickness of paper down and out from behind the bar. She snaps the lever up with a loud clack, opens my door, and grins her way back to her room.

If the lever won't move, the bar won't lift.

So with kite string I wrap and wrap around the bar and the lever, tying them into permanent immobility. Then I sit on my bed and wait, even longer this time. I hear her door open. I feel her studying the problem. I see the white and brown ball of her eye as she peers in around the lever. I am complacent. I have got her this time. I have won. And as I settle into my warm bloodrush of glory, I see the blade of a knife slip silently through the crack between door and jamb, and she saws away at the string. This takes a while. The blade against the tangle of string grates and squeaks. The door rattles some, back and forth with each saw of the blade. As I watch, I feel the fun draining out of me and despair flooding in. Close on the tail of despair, anger edges in. The last string frays in the blade's path, and she snaps the lever up, and opens the door, and gives me a look that seems even sad. I cannot outsmart her. She goes back to her room without a flounce. She knows the game is over. *But if the lever won't move, the bar won't lift.* There must be a way.

For an hour, at least, I work on creating a mess so solid that none of her ploys can dismantle it. The thickness of folded paper, tighter and longer, wadded paper, around the lever and string, and chewing gum holds it all together. And I wait. I wait. I wait. I hear no sound of her for a long time. Then I hear her radio come on and the opening and closing of bureau drawers. I sit on my bed and stare at the mess that has secured my latch and locked me in. I wait and wait more. Finally, she comes out of her room, and as she passes my door on her way to the bathroom, she pauses to pull my lever out of its hole, leaving the mess, the string hanging limply. *If the lever isn't there, there is nothing.*

I am embarrassed and frustrated. I am angry, too angry for the small size of my room. As I jerk stiffly toward the door to rip the mess away and get my lever back, I see my right hand sweep across my bureau, knocking the surface ornaments awry. When all is still, two china horses, a bay and a black, lie shattered on the floor. My heavy, hand mirror lies, its glass unbroken, in the shards and dust of what had been my bank, a gold-painted pig large enough for a 3-year-old to sit on. Now it is gold pieces, with hints of what had been pink flowers painted on its back. Its head lies solid but away from the body. And in the plaster dust and chunks lie silver coins, many 50-cent pieces. I sit on the floor in silence and disbelief. What had started as a game had ended in the wreckage of things I loved. Beyond repair. Wreckage of things loved beyond repair. For a long time I cannot cry. I can only stare. I can feel the wail of a child stuck in my chest. *Look what she made me do! Mama!* But in my mind I hear the words of a non-child. *She did not make you do this. You did it yourself.*

Finally, I begin to assess the damage, to count the dead. I carefully pick up the pieces of pig and limbs of horse, using cotton handkerchiefs from Aunt Edith to help me separate the bay horse from the black from the gold and pink. When all that remains is dust and small unidentifiable white plaster chips, no longer horse or pig, I clean the mess off my latch and get a damp sponge from the bathroom. My lever lies on the floor outside my door. I pick it up, go in and shut the door, and set the lever on my desk. *If the lever isn't there, the bar won't lift.* But as I am wiping up dust and small pieces, my sister sticks her lever into my door, and the bar rises. She has heard a crash. Am I alright?

I have broken two horses and my pig. I nod toward the hankies and box. It is then scalding tears drip from my eyes; like acid, they burn paths along the contours of my face. Cooling to chill, they drip down to my chest. I am ashamed of myself. I have broken things I love. But no wail accompanies the tears. They are silent. My sister squats down and hugs me. I let her. I am not angry with her. I am angry with everything and with myself. She stands up, fetches three boxes from her room, and returns to take carefully my handkerchiefs of shards.

I let her. And for some reason, after this battle of doors, I never go into her room and snoop again. I return to the narrow trail to my office, keeping to my boundaries.

Over the next few weeks, my animals reappear. First the bay, then the black. There are cracks and white spots where chips are missing, but these only make them more precious. I put them on a high shelf with my other more precious objects. But when the pig returns, it is as if he had never been hurt. Missing chips have been reconstructed with plaster or spackling. He is freshly gold, and his flowers are pink and purple and white. His eyes shine blue. They were not noticeably any particular color before. Now they are peacock blue. I do not know for sure if I have my sister to thank. I would not know how to thank her if I tried, just as she would not know how to let me. A stillness grows between us. A silence. Not of anger. Just distance. I think for the first time I recognize the distance. In part it is age and the times. But it is what makes us who we are more than anything else. Needs. Interests. Quirks. Beliefs. Creeds.

In 1966, my sister got married two days before my 13th birthday. I was one of her bridesmaids in yellow satin with a moss-green satin sash and moss-green, dyed Naturalizer shoes with heels. I was forced to shave my legs. I was made to practice in the heels. I was inept and dead serious, as I hobbled down the aisle before my older and elegant cousins. As I passed one pew, someone hissed, "Smile, Betsy." I don't think I did. The wedding passed. The reception was modest but grand. Good food. Good music. Good punch. Inside, my younger sister, 5 and a fine extrovert, spun in dervish windmill circles amongst the dancers. Outside, my yellow satin and moss-green, dyed Naturalizer pumps met February mud in the rainy church driveway, as I made chains of can from the caterers' trash and strung them from the newlyweds' bumper and tucked them neatly out of sight. In the doorway to the reception, women were gathering and passing bags of rice. Purse open, I rose from the mud and went to get my share.

Elizabeth Hodges *is an associate professor at Virginia Commonwealth University where she teaches nonfiction writing at both the undergraduate and graduate levels and is one of two people who directs the Composition and Rhetoric Program.*

Original Friend

Donald Morrill

A year ago, one of my mother's rare, brief letters arrived, bearing in its folds the reason for its being: Tom's obituary. In two column-inches of newsprint, I learned that, at 38, he had died at home of complications from diabetes; that he was a lifelong resident of our hometown in the Midwest; that he was survived by a sister. My mother's letter said he had been cremated the week before, so I was spared a cross-country trip for the service. To be honest, I wouldn't have gone—would have told myself that I couldn't get away, or made some other excuse. Tom and I hadn't spoken in at least a decade, and we hadn't seen each other for longer than that. Yet he had been my closest male companion through childhood, adolescence and beyond. He had been my original friend.

I thumbtacked the obit to the bulletin board near the desk in my study, among—and soon beneath—stalled drafts of poems, post-cards, reminders of things to do. Sometimes I brought myself to find it, and I studied it, looking for some further insight among the few yellowing facts. Memorial contributions, it said, could be made to his church, though Tom had never attended any church in our years as friends. The home address given was not that of his family's house on 33rd Street, two blocks from where I grew up, but of a residence across town, in a more urban, less prosperous neighborhood. When I had known him, he had two much older sisters and an older broth-er—a mythic brother, really—whose existence was demonstrated by a sepia-toned graduation photograph, and who had left behind a conflict with Tom's late father years before, never to return. Legend further asserted that this brother taught at the school back East attended by the Kennedy children. Had one of Tom's sisters and his brother died in the years since we had last talked? Or was this surviving sister the only sibling with whom he still had contact, given his history of familial conflicts?

There was also a photograph: Tom in his familiar aviator glasses, leaning into the frame, portrait-studio style, and looking off toward some horizon beyond the words surrounding his image. There was the burry, bristly, enviably unmanageable hair tapered and parted. There were the faint pencilings of a mustache he had first tried to grow at 15, and the clear, satiny complexion—infant flesh—bearing the slight shadow on the cheek, no doubt his ineradicable red. He didn't smile. He never smiled in pictures, because he was cute and frail of frame, a runt, and had always been so. And he was desperate to be taken seriously—perhaps to take himself seriously—and to be seen as a man, worthy of his brother's legend. He might also have withheld his smile here because his diabetes had cost him several front teeth by his mid-20s. It was impossible to tell how recently the picture had been taken. He had always looked like a boy.

Besides the gravity in the announcement of his death, I kept confronting the crucial absences outlined by these details. Had he died alone? Was it sudden? Had he really gotten religion? Why was he living in such reduced circumstances? Did he have anyone in his life? I envisioned a ramshackle, buff-brick rooming house surrounded by commercial parking lots on the fringe of downtown, and within it a dim, chilly apartment that housed stacked, grimy dishes and tossed clothes, the enduring shambles of a bachelorhood renewed by a divorce more than a decade before. The chill in that apartment clamped down and squeezed the pity up in me—an unjustifiable pity, of course, for a life I had no right to judge as pathetic and somehow failed, though it appeared so.

At the time of our last talk, Tom still lived at the 33rd Street house. In fact, he had just inherited it after his mother's death from a fall we both knew—but would not say—vodka had encouraged. He was thinking of selling the place, and he'd called me to see about the prospects of moving to the town where I then lived in Florida. He sounded eager to start a new life. The county sheriff's office still employed him as a photographer and uniformed clerk—jobs he had always glorified by intimating that they also involved undercover work which had to be kept scrupulously vague. He thought the Sunshine State might be the place to pursue his long-held aspiration for a career as a real law enforcement officer.

He also sounded shy, nearly embarrassed, as he asked if it was possible to stay at my apartment for a few days. A graduate student, I shared a small, one-bedroom unit in a refurbished carriage house with my girlfriend at the time. Though I was surprised and genuinely pleased to hear from him, the mild apprehension in my "sure, no problem" must have struck him square and fortified any reluctance he had felt in calling me. We joked and reminisced, and hung up after promising to talk at the end of the week, when he had made his travel arrangements to Florida. We never spoke again.

Why didn't I pick up the phone when the week passed with no call? Why did neither of us make the gesture? I believed, somehow, that further contact with me would pain him—undoubtedly a rationalization for my own paralysis, or indifference. Yet his silence testified to a distance neither us could broach alone, solitary as we seemed to ourselves in the remains of our friendship, most of which was memory. Had he been as relieved—cruelly relieved—as I to be free of our contact?

The selling of the 33rd Street house touched me as a poignant but inevitable farewell, a necessary transformation. When visiting my parents in the years after Tom and I did not call back, I often drove by it, noting, as in times past, that his car stood in the driveway or was absent—until one day I passed to see different cars parked there, new aluminum siding and window frames, and two children playing on a new swing set out front. Original friends don't choose each other so much as they are tossed together by fortune, and they stay together—even if they are not ideal mates—because their world is small and their alternatives few, and the possibility of questioning and choosing their places in life remains obscured by the naturalness of the way things seem. I don't remember where, or how, we met as children, though it must have been in the local public kindergarten. My first memories of Tom, however, occupy the 33rd Street house and surrounding property. The place became the spiritual center of our friendship, where we learned about intimacy and limits.

That house was not so much my second home as a new world where I could escape the wrenching and embarrassing conflicts in my family. Though not appreciably larger than our two-story place, it seemed richer, more refined and exotic—with a stone fireplace in the living room and built-in, floor-to-ceiling, mahogany bookshelves jammed with forgotten hardback novels; wainscoting in the dining room and beveled glass in the doors; an enclosed front porch mystically called the solarium; and upstairs, a laundry chute. According to Tom, his father had once headed a large construction company in the area before an associate betrayed and ousted him; that was why Tom was born in Australia during a sojourn at a building project and why the older neighbors called him "Dinkum," a nickname at which he scowled frequently. It was also why his father then worked as a welder, he said, and why his parents had to sell off the large acreage that had once surrounded the house, on which a school and some of the neighborhood stood.

I was not a second son at Tom's house because Tom was not so much a son himself as he was a late-arriving, "accidental" obligation to an older, busy, troubled couple. His willfulness and their weariness gradually removed him from the usual parental oversight. Thus, he and the house also embodied a kind of early freedom I might never have discovered on my own. For instance, Tom introduced me to worldly pleasures on one of my innumerable sleepovers. We must have been 10, perhaps 11 years old. His siblings had long before grown up and moved out, and his parents were at work. We had watched "rassling" on television with Tom's grandfather—a failing, crusty, genial man who drank cough syrup and smoked crooked, rum-soaked cigars, and who would die within the next year. Grandfather abed, Tom opened the windows of his room, pulled out a crumpled pack of cigarettes and three Playboy magazines. We sat drenched in the peeled white glow of a bare light bulb. I declined the offer of a cigarette, as I would for a few more years. Tom smoked lavishly on his bed, his nose runny and glistening from manifold allergies, his fingernails uncut and filthy as they would be into adulthood. He'd gazed aplenty at the magazines and reclined in his sophistication. I had never seen such things before, and I did not know they were supposed to be "dirty." I hovered over the images, somewhere in that erotic zone of adolescence just before the first full-force erection arrives with clear neural instructions. A pure, sweet urge held me in a fine mesh of fascination. I remember one image: a woman standing in a red Corvette, her blonde hair flying, bare-breasted, wearing what I believe were white cotton panties. I turned back to her over and over, uncertain why I was drawn to her chest and that one cloaked region. I would look at other such images later, but never as I did on that night.

Tom relished these moments. He liked being the first and being in the know. His proud suavity crowned him like his cigarette smoke. He wore it the day he brought home his snare drum from his first lesson and instructed me in how to hold the sticks, casual about the ways of junior high school band members. He wore it when we hunched over cherry Cokes at the neighborhood drugstore as the older guys—who all knew him because of his sisters—talked about their cars and jobs and dates. He wore it partly because, like the smoke, it could not last long. He was too clumsy, too vulnerable. He didn't finish things. After a time as a thundering band member, he retired his drum. The drugstore studs often gave us rides in their muscle cars, but they also called Tom "Dinkum Stink'm." He sensed I could see these debacles, yet he also perceived that part of me was a great fan of his posturings, his cool, however much it was incommensurate with his station in the world. A simple stability in me approved of his comical swagger, and inflated it and, at the same time, declared it harmless—though, at some level, Tom seemed always to have been harming himself.

We were partners of a sort, even when in the company of friends our age. After his day in the local public school and mine in the Catholic, we swept through imaginary adventures, pretending to be secret agents. We played pick-up football and playground baseball. We lolled through the summer, sitting on his porch in the night odor of cut grass and looking at downtown lights in the distance. Car crazy, we built model racers relentlessly, some in imitation of those on posters plastered across our bedroom walls, accumulating huge stocks of spare parts and customizing paraphernalia. In the old summer house behind the garage—a single oak room, with an attic, that once housed the acreage caretaker—we cleared away stored furniture and rubbish and established a place to build and store our models. With a black marking pen, we drew a sign on a sheet of fiberboard and hung it above the door: *Tom & Don's Speed Shop.*

Some time after this, Tom turned to me and announced that his father had cancer and was going to die. He said it quickly, almost matter-of-factly—uneasily, it seems now. I accepted the news without more than a forgettable comment, probably because I didn't know what to say. At 12 or so, I had not known death, though Tom's grandfather had died the year before. A part of me also thought Tom might be lying about his father, to garner my sympathy—though I couldn't see why he would do that. The next several months witnessed his father's transformation from a tall, whiskey-flushed man in khaki coveralls to a stooped scarecrow sucking his last days through a milkshake straw, his few words popping and gargling from a tumorous throat. Remote in his health, he became, in his decline, our odd intimate, especially in his last summer during which Tom's mother worked days as an aide at a nursing home. We would accompany him on errands, he hunching over the steering wheel, barely able to raise his head. We would try to speak softly when in the house or playing at the speed shop, so as not to disturb his lengthening sleeps.

In those long months, Tom, too, began a transformation that seems obvious now but was then obscure. He grew more willful with his mother, more petulant, no doubt out of confusion and sorrow. Repeatedly, his fury sprang at the order of things as he discovered his new powers, often driving himself, and sometimes me, to precipitous emotional edges. For instance, I walked up the driveway one afternoon to rendezvous, as usual, before we began our newspaper routes. Tom and two of our friends stood in what had been the garage—a ramshackle structure with a rotted, gaping roof and sagging red tile walls. To the shock of all present, Tom had swung a sledgehammer at the supporting beams and bricks, toppling the walls. The others had taken whacks while he'd rested, and then he'd resumed. He pounded and pushed with a fierce concentration—the rest of us laughing nervously and glancing around for the trouble that was sure to arrive—until we all stood taller than the surrounding rubble. At nearly that moment, the back door opened, and Tom's father appeared not in his robe but work clothes. In great agony, meager and barely able to move, he must have risen at the sound of the blows and struggled to dress during the wrecking. He shuffled, head down, mute until he stood before us.

"Goddamnit, Tom!" he mumbled almost inaudibly, breathless like a gutshot infantryman in a Hollywood epic. "What do you think you're doing?!"

Tom stared into his father's face. "Well," he replied, his tone oddly light, "we're going to rebuild the thing, but first we have to clear away all this junk."

In the silence thereafter, we waited, stranded, hysterically still, until Tom's father turned and went back into the house.

Later that summer, Tom and I fought as we hadn't before. The circumstances of the conflict are no longer clear, but we ended up shouting at each other in the speed shop. Tom threw boxes of parts, and I broke some models and walked out. I had only marched 20 or so paces when I heard him call to me. I turned to see him pull down our *Tom & Don's Speed Shop* sign and break in it two.

Even now, that gesture pierces the boy I was, partly because I see that it introduced us to an adult truth. A few minutes later, Tom approached me on the front lawn of the nearby school. I had bounded off and sat and wept, ashamed of my tears but unable to restrain them. The breaking of the sign had astonished me. Only now do I have a word to name what I felt: betrayal, on the order of a lover's unfaithfulness. Tom and I talked, and looked at the sky and, eventually, reconciled. We had discovered the risk in our trust of each other. For some months, the speed shop remained in disrepair, until we finally packed up our model-building paraphernalia and took it home and made the place into a clubhouse for all the friends in our circle.

In the fall after Tom's father died, my parents finally allowed me to transfer from the Catholic school to the public school Tom attended. This furthered the changes between us. Since kindergarten, what I knew of public school life derived from Tom's anecdotes and those of a few others. On the first day of class, I entered the seemingly vast junior high building with Tom in the lead. He introduced me to his friends, showed me around. It was vintage, big-time Dinkum, brimming with the frisson of adolescence and the determination to impress.

And I was impressed, though not as he might have wished. With time, it became clear that Tom did not belong to the most elite cliques, as his stories had implied. He was not the great glad-hander and universal mover and knower, but one on the margins of a cruel and utterly clear social structure. I, of course, was a newcomer and a nobody, which may have quickened these insights. Yet, in them, Tom and I also found ourselves in a familiar relationship. Eventually, we ceased any efforts to be with each other at school and saved our friendship for evenings and weekends and summers.

The following year, Tom decided to go out for the wrestling team. He talked of joining the Marines, of becoming a cop, and he thought that if he could excel at one of the lower weight classes, he could build himself up. Throughout the summer, he seemed to be weak and constantly sleepy. Heading for my paper route in the afternoons, I would enter the 33rd Street house without knocking, since his mother was at work, and find him nearly comatose upstairs. I attributed it to his variable hours and general defiance of his mother's enfeebled rule, both of which I encouraged and shared. The required physical for the wrestling team offered a different explanation, however: a severe case of diabetes.

Just as at school, Tom attempted to show me around the hospital during the weeks of his stay there. It was the same facility in which his father had died. As we strolled the hallways, I remembered the night we stood outside his father's room, how when the door opened and his sister ushered him in, we could see his father's bony feet kicking as he thrashed for his last gasps. Tom seemed to have entered another realm that night, and his illness seemed yet another realm. It was beyond me and always present. In the kitchen after he returned home from his stay in the hospital, his mother instructed me and two other friends—all aged 14—in how to prepare and give Tom a special injection, should he lapse into a coma. The needle and the little brown vials stored in the refrigerator bestowed upon us a responsibility which, for the most part, I took seriously and was relieved to ignore.

Fortunately, I never had to administer that injection. I don't know if I would have been able, as cowardly as I am about needles. Once the glamour of his new condition ebbed, Tom carried his illness like arcane knowledge for everyone to regard and for him to deny. In all the days and nights in the 33rd Street house, I rarely saw him give himself his shots. Still, he sometimes used his burden as a means to make us verify our care—either by our asking if it was wise for him to eat a particular food or drink so much alcohol, or by our pretending not to notice. For him—the slightly-built boy now facing an irrevocable slight—there would be no Marine Corps, so he cast himself, however questionably, into a future as a police officer. He also careened between being his body's ally and its vengeful punisher, until his abuses almost seemed the norm.

Tom's obvious vulnerability usually attracted girls, as did his good looks. Though he was sexually active by 15, he generally maintained a delicate silence about the particulars. In high school, for instance, I hitchhiked across town to his girlfriend's house a couple of times. Her parents were out, and she and Tom would occupy a bedroom upstairs for two or three hours, while I sipped gin and listened to music at the bar in the basement, so as not to hear the bedsprings. Afterward, thumbing back, without strain, we spoke of anything but what had transpired. At that time, I was excited and shy about girls, terrified of going even for that first kiss. Others in our group razzed me about it. Perhaps Tom suspected there might be something wrong with me, since I seemed almost catatonic with fear at the come-ons of his girlfriend's friends. He only mentioned the matter once or twice, tangentially. He sensed in me, I think, a fragility he understood, and left it alone.

Eventually, I found a girlfriend, though not a girl Tom knew. I had begun to roam in different arenas. Tom liked to play the rebel at school and rejected any involvement there. I'd been introduced to "popularity" and the system of gestures necessary to access and enhance it. I was becoming a joiner and doer, and a guy known for his wit—something like the figure Tom had once pretended to be—and I was hoping to learn how far I could go by being seen with the right people. Tom and I never discussed this split between us. I would circle back to the 33rd Street house less frequently but with regularity, and we would smoke and drink and hang out, as always. We graduated. I enrolled at the local college. In the room where Tom's grandfather died, I finally cast off my virginity at 19 with an older friend of Tom's future wife.

His marriage that same year to Debbie, a hairdresser, proved ill-fated. He and Debbie moved into a minimalist apartment complex nearby and arranged their few belongings. Their early life there brimmed with TV evenings and decent home-cooked dinners, and they exuded an enthusiasm that seemed to infect my girlfriend and me. For a short time, she and I talked seriously, and foolishly, of marrying, stimulated most by the thought of picking out furniture together. Tangled in such giddiness, it seems to me now that we most resembled our parents of the World War II generation.

For Tom, marriage was another first, and perhaps the product of a hungering for anchorage against the storms of his own existence. More mature and more reliable, Debbie had lived on her own since her middle teens. She'd worked hard for what she had: a paid-off car, some clothes, cookware and a good sofa. As the months tumbled past, the role of mother and guardian to her young, reckless husband closed slowly around her. Nearly two years had to elapse before she began to realize how much she despised that embrace. By then, she and Tom had moved back to the 33rd Street house, partly to cut expenses. He attended law enforcement classes at the community college and worked at the county jail. I had dropped out of college for a semester, and I paid rent on the room where Tom's grandfather had died and, technically, I'd given away my innocence. Debbie and I became pretty good friends. She was intelligent and talkative, and later she sought in me a confidant for the frustrations with Tom. Marriage had isolated her from old friends, and neither of us felt any connection with Tom's mother, who also lived in the house but who seemed to work night and day, when she wasn't drinking, and who was almost a ghost when she was a presence at all.

Ultimately, I moved out of the 33rd Street house after Tom, in a fury, accused Debbie and me of cheating on him. For some time, he had grown as petulant with Debbie as with his mother, and this incident marked a new level in the escalating conflict that continued until Debbie divorced him a few years later and eventually remarried. His indictment hurt not because I felt betrayal like that on the day he broke the old speed shop sign, but because his desperation awakened in me a pity that had lain dormant since childhood. I had to admit to myself, then, how much we had already left each other behind on our routes to elsewhere. A couple of years before, he had given me what was reputed to be his older brother's Princeton sweatshirt, and I had worn it often. I browsed and read the books lining those beautiful mahogany shelves in the living room, while he never did. Instead, he spoke lavishly about the dangers of his job at the jail, all of the details gleaned, it seemed, from cop shows and, because of this, embarrassing.

Here, my memory of Tom evaporates, except for images from a few late visits and his call to Florida. A blankness remains, on which I try to inscribe some further meaning. In his fantasies, in all his "firsts," Tom sought an outsized, perhaps even heroic life—though he wouldn't have used such terms to describe it. He confronted barriers he probably couldn't name, and neither of us asked many important questions of ourselves during our time together. Who in those years does? I turn now to survey the limits of my own half-vanished life and its untenable, sometimes harmful, ordinary bargains. Among my failings and unrealizable dreams, Tom stands and stares back at me, another "first" for him. Alternately 18, 20, 13, 24, he offers no word about how unfairly or inaccurately I've represented him here, nor any word about the present or the future. Instead, he swaggers, as always, almost on tiptoes. His eyes well with tears from a smashing tackle on the playground. Or he adjusts the badge on his uniform. Though long out of contact with him, I could, while he was in the world, at least wonder what had become of him. The wondering must be different now.

Donald Morrill*'s prose and poetry have appeared in a number of magazines, including Grand Tour, New Virginia Review, The Southern Review, The Kenyon Review and Creative Nonfiction. He was the recipient of The Missouri Review's Editors' Prize for Nonfiction in 1996. The essay "Original Friend" will appear in Morrill's next book, "A Stranger's Neighborhood," to be published in the fall of 1997 by Duquesne University Press as part of the Emerging Writers in Creative Nonfiction book series.*

Vanish Away Like Smoke

Andy Solomon

Mr. Kohlbert locked his hands behind his back and paced in front of the class. "Und sooooooo...," he droned, "Ve haf efry reason to belief dat Columbus vas a Jew."

I paused in the sketch I was drawing of a new 1957 Ford Thunderbird and glanced around the musty classroom. The other students, like me, were all within months, one side or the other, of their 12th birthdays. Their eyes spoke an interest I could not believe was real. After all, it was Sunday, 11 a.m., and like me, they must have wanted to be somewhere else, anywhere but here. I put the rubbery-tasting eraser end of my pencil in my mouth and gazed around at the girls' chests to see if any needed a larger bra than the last time I'd looked, a half-hour before.

I never much minded that week after week I sat sweating in this overheated room listening to what seemed like myths, wishes, legends and lies related as truth. I minded only that their truth seemed so damned important to Mr. Kohlbert, the bald teacher with the grating voice. World War II had ended the year I was born, and I had been told to accept on faith that a German Jew like Kohlbert had suffered in a way I was assured I could never understand, assured by my father, to whom the lies seemed equally crucial, who had lamented often that he too had suffered, been denied that job, a home in that neighborhood, membership in that club, just because his name was Solomon.

Another suffering member of our victimized, martyr race.

"Aha, you see?" my father, I knew, would say with a slight but continuous nod if I chose later to relate this news about Columbus. "Aha, you see?"

I did not see. I had been refused nothing. Being born a Jew had cost me nothing, I valued it at nothing, and I would rather have spent my Sunday mornings playing stickball at Mt. Vernon Junior High.

Only Michael Hirsch and Laurie Beckerman were not looking at Mr. Kohlbert. They looked at each other and at me. Laurie tapped her purse twice. She lifted her index and middle fingers in a V toward her mouth, puckered her full lips, and winked. She'd brought them, the three Kent cigarettes she'd snuck from her mother's pack as she did each Sunday. I winked back and began drawing on the inside back cover of my Jewish history book what I thought Laurie might look like standing on a tree limb with no clothes on, smiling, sweetly naked and dewy, honey-blond strands caressing her face. A few days before, I'd tried to draw Laurie nude in my science notebook during fifth period, and when Carol Buchwald, who sat beside me and told me we were going steady, saw the sketch, I said it was what I thought she'd look like with short hair. She giggled and said, "It would look more like me if you'd make the boobs bigger." Carol took a deep breath, making her left nipple strain against her cashmere.

"I see your point," I said and doubled the size of Laurie's breasts, which made Carol say, "I love you, Andy."

Mr. Kohlbert cleared his throat loudly. He was glaring at me, determined to give my pride in Columbus' religion a jump start. He came to my seat and walked around it. He looked down at me, the fluorescent light glaring off his scalp. "Boys und girls, ven you get back from your break, ve vil discuss de responsibilities ve take on for being God's chosen people," he said and pushed us toward the door with a backhand wave.

"So how 'bout that," said Laurie. She inhaled deeply. She'd been smoking for months now and liked to show off how easy it was, even that week she'd brought her father's Lucky Strikes, to speak with a chest full of smoke. "Columbus was a Jew. 'Stop the boat, boys! It's Friday night, and I can't travel for the next 24 hours.'"

"Go believe that crap," I said. I took a small puff on Laurie's mother's Kent, kept it in my mouth, let it seep out, and tried to draw the smoke into my nostrils. It almost made me sneeze, but I fought the sneeze off before Laurie or Michael could see. I rolled my short sleeves up another inch and leaned casually back against the smudged wall of the boiler room in the synagogue's basement, the basement itself always deserted, a safe grotto in which to sneak our cigarettes.

"You know what that means, Laurie?" said Michael. He stood up straight. I hated when Michael stood up straight. He was 4 inches taller than I and was even talking about buying a razor. He stuck his face right up to Laurie's, inches from the sweet lips I'd licked Bonimo's Turkish Taffy off of in three separate dreams. "The guy who discovered this country was circumsized. Got a clue what that means?"

"Of course, stupid."

"Like hell you do."

"I'll draw it for you, smart ass."

"I'll *show* it to you, cute ass."

All three of us laughed together, then suddenly, together, grew still with fear. Footsteps. The sound was unmistakable, the squeak and scrape on the cement floor, loud against the basement's silence. Too petrified to drop our cigarettes, we let our widened eyes stare at the door. Could someone from the class have stumbled upon this room it had taken even us so long to discover? Would it be Harvey Bloom, the crew-cut brown-noser who told Mr. Kohlbert anything that might ingratiate? Would it be, no it couldn't be, even Kohlbert himself?

"What do I smell here?" It seemed like a full second pause between each bellowed word. A voice that sounded less like it came from a doorway than from a burning bush. Not quite God's, the voice belonged to the man who was as close to God as we could get.

"What's this? What do I smell?" He stood in full view now. His pressed lips made his beard jut out. One eyebrow lifted an inch higher than the other. He raised his arms, and the front of his red robe parted.

"Nothing," said Michael in a voice quivering like Jell-O you'd just tapped with a spoon. "Nothing, Rabbi Weisman."

"Nothing?" he thundered. "It's nothing I smell here, Laurie?"

Laurie looked at her cranberry penny loafers.

Rabbi Weisman glanced down toward her loafers, then back up, scowling at her as if she were a television he'd hit but could not get to stop scrolling. He turned to me, his last hope for confession. He folded his arms, tapping his left hand against his thin right bicep,

rocking back and forth in his squeaky brown wingtips. "*Nu,*
Andrew? You also think I smell nothing?"

It would not be lying to a man, I thought. It would be lying to
God. Kohlbert was one thing, easily dismissed. But the rabbi was no
ordinary man. Like Abraham, like Moses, he and God kept in touch,
they were friends. God was in this room with him, both waiting for
my answer.

"Cigarettes, rabbi."

"Cigarettes!" He flung his arms open. "*Gott in Himmel!*
Cigarettes!" He flung them back across his chest and gasped as if we
had given him a bodily wound.

"Cigarettes, rabbi."

"Your parents know you smoke cigarettes?"

Three heads shook.

"They would approve?"

Three heads shook.

"This time you are very, very lucky. This time I will not tell your
parents, but..." His voice rose and, I knew, was about to chisel something in stone, "You will never, never do this again. Never again!"

"Never, rabbi." "They'd kill me, rabbi." "Thank you, rabbi. We're
sorry." Our voices mingled in lingering fear and relief, and the rabbi
left.

Kohlbert would have told them, I was certain. He'd have called
them before class even resumed. But ours is a merciful God, and He
has asked the rabbi to spare us this time. I told the truth, and He
rewarded me. I will thank Him, maybe even ask my parents if I can
go to services with them this Friday night. I can miss "Life of Riley"
on television this once.

It was Monday, the following night. I stretched out and lay back
against the sofa. My right foot rested high on my left thigh, and I
opened and closed my new Flap Jacks from Thom McAn. Carol had
said they were boss. I was thinking about putting taps on them but
doubted I was tough-looking enough to justify the image. Maybe I
could get away with it if I were Italian.

I had finished all my pot roast and even the carrots and was eating an ice cream sandwich. I licked the edges slowly, trying to get all
the ice cream out and be left with only the delicious chocolate sides.

On the television screen George Burns was holding a cigar and explaining Gracie's actions to the camera, and I was laughing as hard as at their previous week's muddle. Outside the window the season's final snowstorm began easing up. I grew worried. Even on a snowy day, my father's trucks should all be in, and he should be home. It was only a half-hour before bedtime, and I wanted to tell him about the A-minus I'd gotten that morning on my social studies term project.

The doorknob grunted warmly, and the apartment door swung open. My father stomped the snow from his shoes and entered. He placed his fedora crown down on a magazine to catch the melting snow.

I waved high and wide, my arm a metronome. "Hi, Dad. I got great news for you."

My mother kissed his cheek. He patted her arm absently and walked past her, directly to the television, which he turned off.

"Andy, the rabbi called me at work."

My heart did something gymnastic. "He called you?"

"Of course he called me. Smoking! You think he shouldn't have called me?"

"But he said he wouldn't."

"Are you questioning the rabbi?"

"But he gave his word. He promised. He's the rabbi. He's supposed to be holy."

"It's you who's in trouble here, you schmuck, not the rabbi."

I stared at a painting across the room, a portrait of my mother in a rose-colored blouse, but my eyes saw only the rabbi standing in the sanctuary, leading us in prayer, holding against his ribs the scrolls descending to him from Moses himself, cradling them so lovingly you'd think Rabbi Weisman had hand-copied them. He told. He lied. He wears robes and interprets the Torah and has a gray beard and reads Hebrew faster than I can read English. He promised, and it was a lie.

"You will go to bed this instant...."

"But 'Wyatt Earp's' coming on."

"This instant."

"I got my social studies..."

"This instant! Tomorrow we will discuss your punishment. But this you can believe: You're in big trouble."

I shuffled to my room. Even through the Flap Jacks I felt the coldness of the hardwood floor. I tugged my clothes off and threw them in the corner. One sock landed against the white baseball Jim Gilliam had fouled off the year before. An usher had been dusting a seat to my right, high in the first base upper deck at Ebbets Field, when Gilliam sent the ball soaring toward me. My father leaped up and snared it with the ease of an angel catching a star. He had tousled my hair through my Brooklyn Dodger cap and slipped the ball into my windbreaker pocket. That ball was my favorite possession.

I pulled the bleachy-smelling sheet up to my nose in the darkness and could feel my breath trapped against it, coming in irregular stutters. My skin felt bristling and prickly. My parents seemed to be debating in the living room, but the words were muffled by a pounding in my ears. I lay a long time watching the shadows drift across the ceiling, cloudy ink-blot forms growing steadily more ominous. My father's punishments were never pleasant, but they always seemed fair, even to me. It would not be so bad that I was in trouble. But I was not the one I feared for. I lay awake a long time, hearing the flattened voices, feeling my own moist breath, staring into a deepening darkness that began to invade me, under the growing horror that the one who was in trouble was God.

Andy Solomon *was born in Mt. Vernon, N.Y., educated at the University of Pittsburgh, and teaches at the University of Tampa where he designed the creative writing major.*

Bloodtalk
Daynotes of a Psychotherapist

Kay E. Morgan

*I've kept journals for 40 years. Over the past eight years, I've been filling journals with **patient** talk, quotes from correspondence with friends and with my son, who currently resides in a federal penitentiary.*

***Patient** talk is language that most closely matches what my mother called **bloodtalk**: talk that matters, throbs, quivers, rivets; that is both colloquial and elegant. Talk with bite. Talk that struts its stuff. As a psychotherapist, I am fortunate to be able to hear the gorgeous language of real people.*

Errors and corrections, errors and corrections. So far as I can tell, that's what psychotherapy is all about. Yesterday a 5-year-old girl became so angry when I tried to engage her in conversation that she tore off all her clothes and threw them in my face.

"It's not in my talk!" she yelled. "Quit talking to me! It's not in my talk!"

She was much smarter than I; of course it wasn't in her talk. The clothes throwing was "her talk," that was the story.

Sometimes, lots of times, I don't know what to do. And it's not even just with clients. Should I have left the movie theater on Sunday when the film broke? I sat there for 45 minutes, slumped in my seat. I didn't call my housebound friend yesterday; why not? And, for publicity's sake, I gave a newspaper interview in which I pretty much laid out my life for all the world (Bremerton, Wash.) and all my clients to read.

My therapist friends couldn't believe my *insousiance*, as one of my older male peers called it. Well, what to do? Each day seems wholly separate from other days. Each month seems so, too. Conventional courtesies sometimes feel right, sometimes wrong. Last week, I didn't have any "double-ups," so I wore the same outfit every single day. "This job is great," I thought. "Nobody knows."

"You know who's got blood?" my mother once asked me.

She used the word blood in various ways, as in *character* or *smarts*.

"Gorgeous George, the wrestler, that's who. His blood is hot as peppers. I'd like to be a scientist and compare Gorgeous George's blood to, say, Liberace's. Sure, they both wear fancy costumes, but there's a difference. Liberace smiles from *above* his belt. Gorgeous George smiles from *beneath* his belt."

I wasn't in love with Gorgeous George as a child, although he made an impression. I was in love with Jerry Lee Lewis. "But he did icky things with his young cousin!" my girlfriends all said. "All the better," I said. My girlfriends liked boys with one syllable names who were just dumb lugs with a certain cuteness. I didn't know much, but I knew sexy, and Jerry Lee was the epitome of sexiness. Even when I see him now, old, wrinkled and slower, not able to get his leg up on the piano keys anymore to pound out a chunk of wild sound, I still stop whatever I am doing and watch with rapt attention.

"But how can *talk* work? If talk worked, my life would be great; hell, I've been talking all my life," said a prospective client on the phone.

Partly I agree, but mainly I don't. Past and present always want to rise up and speak, and the speech they want to use is what my mother meant when she said bloodtalk. If you and I, together, can meet inside our histories, tarnished and bloodied and threadbare as they may be, if we can meet and speak out our histories until they become, through our words, flags of victory, then the sleepless devils of yesterday will disappear, and we can finally turn to the passion of everyday sustenance. At least today that is what I believe.

When it comes to words, the world offers us everything we need. Each conversation, each "overheard something" is a great gift. This afternoon I went to a thrift store to buy old keys to use on a collage.

As I was leaving, I heard the man who stood behind me ask the clerk, "What do you suppose she intends to do with all those keys?"

"Who knows," mused the clerk. "Some people just like to have extra sets of entitlements."

The first time Kevin was in jail I visited him twice a week. It was county jail. He was in for taking off during probation. He'd gone to Hollywood. For six months, we received collect calls from various California phone booths, and five times the local police came to our door, demanding, "Where is your son?"

"Somewhere in L.A.," we'd say. "Look, this is all we know."

Once, one of the policemen winked at me and said, "Well, maybe we'll catch him in the movies."

Kevin called to say he'd seen Karl Malden in a supermarket. The week after that, it was Burt Reynolds on the beach.

"It's really important not to bother them," Kevin said. "They have enough on their minds already."

"Oh, Kevin," I remember saying. "Come back. I'll help you with the system. Things are always better if you face them."

That was the therapist-me talking. The other part, the part that wanted my own entitlements, disowned my therapist words. "Stay there, Kevin," I thought. "Just stay."

"And I may as well tell you that I'm sexually repressed and so are all my friends, which makes it convenient and inconvenient at the same time. We're also all National Honor Scholars, so it's not for lack of brains; in fact our brains are probably our most outstanding problem. I mean, if you cut off our heads and managed to keep them going somehow, well, we wouldn't notice a difference. I mean it! Life would go on like always. Just once, I'd like to start thinking about what's between my legs. At this point in my life, if someone else was wearing my pants, I wouldn't even notice."

—5 o'clock patient

"I'm afraid to act like everything is fine. When I was a kid, I lived in 'Crazy.' It was only through my mother's 'Come to Jesus' moods that Crazy left. Otherwise it was knives, knives, knives and not for cutting meat.

"I need to learn how to say 'Stop it!' and then I need the next part to happen—I need it to *stop*. I want to write to my older brother and at the end say, 'P.S. I faxed your home phone number to the State Pen. I told them what you did to me. Have fun! Love, ——'"

—3 o'clock patient

We speak with several voices, out of several selves. Psychotherapy allows people to naturally enter—and experience—the power of poetic speech. Because I seek the personal, caring modes of psychotherapy, as opposed to the "scientific helper" modes, I could easily make poems out of patient talk. It's raw, crude poetry, and not one of my patients would claim it for its infectious spontaneity, but like Ray Bradbury said, "Oh, it's limping crude hard work for many, with language in their way." The passionate, the dramatic, the mysterious, the mystic—so many individual elements lend themselves to that moment of truth called poetry.

Here is a "found poem" taken directly from this afternoon's 5 o'clock patient notes:

Last night I dreamed
I lived a time called Dogtime.
A giant emerging eye asked,
Have you received your dignity?
Stabs of memory
Always come for me
That way, at night.
Now, I believe myself.
Open windows.
Bathroom doors.
Grandma and Grandpa.
Every night one of them
Comes to kill me.
I am tired of running away.

Come home, come home.
You are the lonely blossom.
If I stand half in your light,
Half out, you invite the silence
That follows silence.

I'd rather read regular people's poems than most poems by real poets. I'd also rather eat macaroni and cheese or tuna casserole than fresh salmon or abalone. I'd rather keep my house looking fairly neat and know that every one of my drawers is an incredible mess than clean my drawers. I eat with my fingers whenever possible. And, all too often, I'd rather lie than tell the truth.

Melanie, my 10 o'clock patient, sits cross-legged on my striped office couch and muses out loud:

"Spring is the hard bowl, cracking. White chicken legs and red plump worms. Tulips aren't beauties the first day. Nature says 'Yes' and marches on, chest stretched, without excuse. Why did it take me until 10 minutes after the hour to arrive here? I will always be the last one to don shorts in the summer. I will always be the last one jumping into the lake."

Language walks around my office all day; all I need to do is sit, and *whoosh*, it comes, and with it always come thoughts of my mother and her insistence on bloodtalk. "Bloodtalk matters," she said, "so watch out."

I watched out. As a child, the only kind of talk I did not want to hear was what my mother called bloodtalk. It scared me; I thought it was...well, bloody. Too direct. Too in-your-face. I even remember making a vow to live and speak as smoothly and surface-ly as possible.

So how did I come to this, 38 years later? Living in the face of raw emotions, my own and others? Maybe, as I keep paying attention to my clients' raw language and my delight in hearing it, I can come to an understanding of how I came from *there* to *here*.

My son writes me from the Federal Penitentiary in Phoenix, Ariz., where he is serving time for bank robbery:

"How come you never really seem to believe me when I tell you it wasn't your fault? What do you read that you keep on believing it was your fault? Didn't your psychology classes teach you anything, or was it their fault that you think it's your fault? I don't like it when you blame yourself. You wouldn't know how to rob 15 banks if your next meal depended on it. Stop reading guilt books. Stop talking to guilt people. I have seen so much terror in the past four years that I hate to think of you terrorizing yourself, so stop it. Happy Mother's Day to you both, Mom and Dad. Funny, but Dad's my mother, too, and I love you both. —Kevin."

Years and years ago, a man exposed himself to me in a local drugstore. He exposed himself at the same time he spoke to me, and he spoke in such an engaging and friendly manner that I talked with him for quite a while before I noticed the *something pink* which hung out of his pants. I was holding two packs of gum, one Baby Ruth candy bar and a tube of Chapstick. When I finally got the picture, I screamed, threw everything at the man's penis, which looked so dramatically disconnected from everything else in the place, and ran out of the store. I have always wondered whether my reaction further excited him or if it wounded him.

An 18-year-old male patient says, "I think feminism is a horrible thing for parents to teach little boys. Women want you to be sensitive and sweet, but they also want something more. If you've been as well-trained as I have been on the subject of feminism, that something more is tantamount to rape. Being a feminist male is like being a battery-operated car. Sure, you can get to the market, but that's about it."

"She's that 800-pound gorilla who knows she can sit anywhere she damn well wants to in my head."
—4 o'clock patient

My son is thinking about ancestors. He writes, "Everyone is coming back. Grandpa Anderson, who ran off with the Thanksgiving turkey, tell me about him. And Mannie. Manuel. He belonged to Aunt Rosita, didn't he? Did he really *belong* to her?

"You know, one of the banks I robbed had a teller who looked just like Aunt Jan's daughter, Christie. I got turned inside out so that I thought she *was* Christie, and it knocked me off my regular track. I usually said, 'Give me the money in your drawer, please' and 'Thank you, Ma'am,' but this time I just stood there, brain twirling like a top. It's easy to steal from strangers, especially after taking that bank tellers course I took, but to steal from a cousin, that wasn't in the training.

"So I said real low so as not to scare her, or, of course, bring undue attention because this was my 10th and I hadn't yet run out of banks, I whispered, 'Christie.' She looked at me. I whispered her name again, and then said, 'Christie, I'm really sorry, but I'm gonna have to rob you because I'm here at the end of the line and I've got to make some sort of transaction and I don't have any money. I'm sorry. Listen, I don't want to brag, but look me up. I'm in some magazines. Don't tell Mom, though, she'll hear the news when they get me, and they will. Just please give me the money in your drawer, please. I don't have a gun.' She gave me the money in the drawer, then she said, 'My name's not Christie.'"

Kevin—again:
"The other night my cellie and I read 'Hamlet' to each other. He'd never seen old books, and you know how sometimes in those really old books the 'S's' look like 'F's?' So when it was his turn to read I'd have to turn my face and hit the pillow hard because he'd read it like the 'S' really was an 'F.' *'To fleep, perfance to dream, aye, theref the rub.'*
Love,
Kevin"

One day, while I was searching for a straight black skirt, the shop owner, a lovely Southern woman, brought another woman over to meet me. The owner is known to be a good conservative woman, and I had always appreciated her friendliness. I had not, however, told her much of anything about my life.

"This is Kay Morgan," the shop owner said, "One of the very finest people you will ever know. Kay is one of my favorite people. She's talented and sweet and, well, just one of the good people! And,

I have heard," she went on, "That you are going to Phoenix this weekend. What kind of exciting thing will you be doing there?"

"I'll just be visiting my son," I said, hoping she would ask no more.

"Oh, how exciting!" the shop owner said. "He must be a wonderful boy. What is he doing in Phoenix?"

Her tall, lovely friend looked at me and smiled. They both stood and looked at me and smiled. I cleared my throat, trying to think of all the options. Finally, I just went for it.

"There's a federal penitentiary in Phoenix," I said. "My son is in there."

The friend took a step back, but the shop owner didn't miss a beat. She grabbed my hand, patted it several times, gave me a warm hug, and said, "And so are some of our finest politicians."

The anniversary of my mother's birth. So enmeshed were we, sleeping together, battling together, taking pills together, that one day she glanced at our images in the bathroom mirror and said, "Uncanny. I've given birth to myself."

Her words gave me the creeps. I didn't mind being like her, no matter what she did or where she did it, but she made it sound like I was her. One person, not two. I looked at myself in the mirror, then I pinched myself hard and held out my arm for her inspection.

"It's me that hurts," I said. "Not you."

And she said—and this is the kind of thing she always said, and always it was a surprise—she said, "I think people are afraid, more than anything else, of other people."

She turned and left me standing alone in the bathroom. I smiled at myself in the mirror, but the image that smiled back did not feel like a friend.

Still thinking about my mother. One of the last times we were all together, my mother, father and I—meaning one of the last times I remember before she died—my father ate a cheese sandwich in the living room, came into the kitchen where my mother and I were sitting, turned on the kitchen overhead light, and said, "Well, things are perfect again. As long as we have good food and each other and a roof over our heads, things are pretty near perfect."

My mother poured herself a drink and glowered at the two of us.

"If this is the best it gets," she said, "I'm gone."

Nothing had ever prepared me for this, the utter sense of lost-ness. We were all lost in a fog. I mean literally, not metaphorically.

Long gone, long gone, like a turkey through the corn, as the old song goes. And then she went.

I was 19 when I first entered therapy. My doctor wore a blue tie with white ducks swimming across it in lines. He must have been in his 50s. However old he was, I was very much in love with him, and I hated it when his wife answered the door to usher me into his office. I wanted him to do all the ushering. In the center of his office stood a table holding a white bust. My parents had forbidden me to take high school psychology classes, and I had not yet been to college. I had no idea who this bust-person was. I thought it might be my doctor's father, that perhaps, in this grand old neighborhood of Tacoma, Wash., people held on so tightly to family values that he had chosen to revere his father in this way. If I said something particularly insightful or particularly lacking in insight, my doctor would turn to the white bust, make a little nod, then turn to me and ask, "Well, and what do you suppose The Master would say about that?" The nodding part threw me; all I could think of to do was nod back. So I'd do a little nod and shrug my shoulders; damn if I know, I'd think, but not say. One day he gave me hundreds of old Saturday Reviews plus a book by Ashley Montague, and I figured out who the bust was. It was Sigmund Freud. Never in my life have I seen or pretended such reverence.

"I've come up with a few predictions," says my last patient of the day, a rosy-cheeked young man who can't yet look at me, but who sits closer and closer to the center of the couch. His words excite me. "In the future all men will all wear fedoras. Corporations will openly promote and pursue greater and greater amounts of anxiety. In the future, an existential theology will form a rigid orthodoxy which will excommunicate all people who believe in anything at all."

We fly to Phoenix to visit Kevin in the Arizona Federal Penitentiary. All the inmates wear ironed khaki shirts and pants, making them look like Marines. We, the visitors, are the ones who look like the bank robbers, the counterfeiters, the drug warlords. It takes about an hour of sitting next to him before my son can be touched. In one of last year's letters he wrote, "Sometimes at night I get so hungry for tenderness I take my left hand gently in my right hand and hold it, as if it were someone else's." That letter, it broke my heart. This morning while I wait for Kevin to walk out of the convict door, I can't help but overhear a good-looking Italian guy murmuring to his female friend, "Oh baby, baby, there's gonna be bad news in my dreams tonight, no doubt about it." *Bad news in my dreams tonight.* What a wonderful thing to say.

Kevin walks out and looks around. I stand and move slowly towards him.

There are rules here. Don't run. Dress appropriately (but many of them don't, and I think it must drive their men nuts). Don't call out. A felon doesn't look at another felon in the eye. A felon doesn't look at another felon's wife or girlfriend. You can kiss at the beginning and ending of each visit. You can't bring anything to your felon.

Kevin sees me, smiles, we meet, hug and sit. Ceiling cameras rotate. Guards mill about. Kevin and I talk in short bursts for the first hour. How's it going? How's it going with Dad? How's it going in here? Who's he? What'd he do to get in here? Look at that cute little kid, isn't that the cutest little kid?

After about an hour I ask if I can put my hand on his back. He nods yes. I lift my hand and place it gently on his back. I touch my son. The feeling is almost too intense. I want to run and sob. I want to lie down in a church, hold my breath forever, dive to the bottom of the ocean.

My mother was an incurable, incredibly loyal racist. Part Canadian-Indian, all poor, most of her siblings ended up in North Dakota's Jamestown asylum. My mother not only hated blacks, Chinese, Japanese, British and Jewish people, she also hated authority figures (judges, lawyers, police, the president, senators, representatives and high school principals) and the rich (anyone who lived in a two-story house, had drapes, maybe a shower and especially, damn them, a swimming pool).

I was astounded, therefore, the day she told me that Dr. Martin Luther King talked bloodtalk—and that she called him Doctor.

"Teddy Roosevelt's 'Walk softly and carry a big stick' isn't bloodtalk, hell, it's common sense. But that Martin Luther King, when he said that 'I had a dream' speech about all the little children, that was good. It had beat, and it gave me the shivers. He can't help it he's black and brilliant, although that non-violence garbage he keeps harping on is just so much cowdung, but maybe his mother didn't teach him right. Anyway, that Dr. King, he talks bloodtalk, and he's big enough to throw a good punch if anybody besides me bad-talks his mother."

At last, Kevin has been transferred close to home; five hours of driving time away, to FCI Sheridan, Ore. Jim drives while I write in my journal. We're penitentiary bound!

Sitting in the lobby. The place is sparkly clean. Nice as Phoenix, loads nicer than Terminal Island. My journal, anchor to the regular world, will soon be taken from me and locked away in a steel locker.

Here is what we do: Make a run for the desk, grab a visitor's form before they disappear, fill it out. Remember our convict's number: No. 20842-086. Remember our convict *is* a number. Put down the number of our car license, the car's make and year, our address, our name, our relationship to our convict. Do everything right. At Terminal Island, that hellhole of dirt and bribery, I once wrote my name in the wrong place and was detained for three hours. Grab a paper clip. Attach your driver's license to your form with the paper clip. Rush it to the guard's desk—we want to be the first to get in.

Sit down. Look around. Don't stare. Once again, smile if smiled at, otherwise, don't. Except for children. We can smile at them, but be careful, not too big a smile.

Three Hispanic men. Ten or 11 Caucasian men and women. Everyone is between the ages of 20 and 50 except for one grandmother, leathered and tough, her little grandson glued to her side. Perhaps the man in the T-shirt that reads "Shipfitters Do It Better" is her son.

A beautiful young woman leans forward to smooth her nylons and—no, no!—her right breast falls out. She sits up; she does not know. Her breast is so small, so perfect, the top of her dress is lacy and low. There is no wind indoors; she cannot feel a thing. Nobody says a word. The social protocol is so strict, what should we do? Ahhh, God!—here comes the little boy. He breaks away from his tough-looking grandmother and runs directly to the young woman; he takes his hand and bashes it into her bare breast. "Tit! Tit! Tit!" the little boy yells.

The grandmother gets to her feet and whacks him two or three times. Now the child's father screams at him, yanks him away from the grandmother, hits him on the bottom, and calls him a "fucking little creep."

The young woman is crying. I move closer. I try to soothe her by asking how far she has come.

What's going on here could have serious repercussions between the prisoners being visited. This is dangerous stuff. These people don't seem to understand that the relationships between visitors must mirror the code of conduct between inmates; that words uttered between visitors can become debts of respect between convicts and that debts of respect can be deadly.

I will not tell Kevin about the tit incident. The word *breast* may be whispered but not spoken aloud. Here, words like *killer, Hitler, gun, sex, racist, Jesus, Hispanic, black, Jew* and *death sentence* are not spoken. It may or may not be appropriate even to say *Caucasian* or *white*. For some reason, *Indian* is usually OK, although I don't know about *Native American*.

Don't worry about not knowing what to say. Your convict will tell you. One thing: Bloodtalk is not spoken here.

Kay E. Morgan is a psychotherapist who has written in journals for 40 years. She teaches journal writing at conferences around the country and has published several stories in the North American Review, as well as Calyx and Changes.

Cy Twombly

Alec Wilkinson

Cy Twombly, the austere and enigmatic expatriate painter who recently had a retrospective at the Museum of
Modern Art, hates watching his paintings leave the house. He imag-
ines the movers in Rome, where he lives, crossing the street with a
canvas and someone on a motor scooter driving through it, like a
stunt in a circus. Twombly lives on a narrow street, in a palazzo that
was built in the 17th century. On the morning the summer before
last that a number of paintings departed for the Modern all the shut-
ters in the house were closed against the heat. While the movers
wrapped the pictures in plastic and placed them in carrying frames,
Twombly walked from one high-ceilinged room to another.
Occasionally, he dabbed a handkerchief at his forehead and the back
of his neck.

Twombly is 70. He is tall and long-limbed and loose-jointed. He
walks with small steps, and his stately progress gives an impression of
thought and abstraction. Pacing the hallways of the palazzo in the
blue-gray light he looked ghostly. Or, with the gravity of his movements, like a cardinal in his chambers. It took perhaps half an hour
to wrap each painting and settle it into its frame. Some of the paintings had been turned to the wall for years, ever since they last
returned from shows.

While Twombly examined a folder of reproductions of the
works he was sending to the museum, his son Allesandro and his
assistant Nicola discussed how to turn the last painting. Nicola stood
on one side of the frame, and Allesandro stood on the other.
Twombly had his back to them; he had laid the folder of reproduc-

tions on a sculpture stand. Nicola said, "Here comes another painting, Cy." Twombly was leafing through the pages. All he said was, "Do it." Saying, "Ready...OK...now," Nicola and Allesandro began lifting the frame. They had turned it perhaps a quarter of the distance it had to travel when it began tilting toward the floor. Nicola drew his breath in sharply, and Twombly wheeled around. Nicola said, "It's all right, it's all right," and he and Allesandro quickly steadied the frame. Twombly stood watching them then. As the surface of the canvas finally came into view, he smiled and said quietly, "Now, *there's* a painting."

In New York, at the museum, several months later, people stood in front of the painting—it is called "Olympia"—and said:

"Clive wanted to introduce me to someone—he was very sweet about it—and said it was a great friend, college roommate or something, I don't know, and I had to say, but Clive, *I went out with his older brother!*"

"This makes me think of aliens."

"I'm not supposed to be doing this. The doctor said so—no stimulation, you know—but I can't sit in my room all the time."

"*This* I could live with. Not the other one, the gray one. The gray one made me anxious."

"It's so, so..."

"This means a lot to me. I had a postcard of this for years on my desk."

"How are you supposed to look at this? I mean, where is the focus?"

"How does he know when it's finished?"

"It's about nothingness."

"It's about what's inside the heart."

"This sort of makes slight fun of art in a way, right? It says, 'Don't take art too seriously'?"

"I don't take them to *drive*. Oh my God, no, I take them to make me *feel* better."

"Jackson Pollock, right?"

"Pollock poured paint."

"Well, it looks like he poured some paint over here."

"It's not supposed to make sense, right?"

"It's about urban decay, is it not?"

"Isn't the ideal of art to help us to learn? This is frustrating to me. It's supposed to be about communication, and he's not communicating."

A thin young man, wearing a red shirt and black jeans and carrying a pack over his shoulder, stood in front of the painting. He took a small notebook from his pocket. He wrote: "Olympia. 1957. Has a myth as subject, or object, whatever. Dynamic Greek goddess. Lots of heart in it. It gives me a feeling of glory and worship."

Alec Wilkinson *is the author of five books, including "Big Sugar" and "A Violent Act." Since 1980, he has been a writer on the staff of The New Yorker.*

Home

Kathryn Rhett

*A*t home I sat in a chair by the window, watching Frisbee players in the park, cars pulling into the gas station. The hospital had been a natural setting for a crisis, its waiting areas filled with worried relatives who blinked at our footsteps then retreated back into themselves when they saw we weren't doctors. We walked from my maternity room to the intensive care nursery to the cafeteria to the offices of social workers and neonatologists. It wasn't abnormal to feel upset in a hospital. Our baby daughter, born the night before, had been diagnosed with meconium aspiration syndrome and persistent fetal circulation, her lungs constricted closed after delivery complications. We watched the ventilator puff her chest, the only visible movement of her body, which was paralyzed with muscle relaxants. We watched and waited, her illness a variation on our rapidly expanding idea of the birth experience.

I hadn't minded too much that the other women in the maternity room had their babies parked bedside in plastic bassinets, because mine was right down the hall with other babies who breathed through turquoise tubes, attended by other mothers who shuffled in cotton gowns. But to arrive home—after a stop at the dirty Haight Street McDonald's, as if we couldn't stand to be in our apartment just yet—without Cade was a blow. The car seat waited by the door. The tiny yellow sleeper suit and blanket were still wrapped in a plastic bag, stuffed in the duffel that now sat, zipped shut, at the foot of our bed.

The crib lay in pieces on the floor of the nursery, which we also used as a study. We hadn't wallpapered a room, made curtains, or hung a mobile. Though the middle of my pregnancy went well, it was framed by events that made the chances of a healthy baby feel less than guaranteed: I experienced bleeding in the first trimester and preterm labor at seven months. The baby clothes Betsy had sent were still in boxes. We'd bought diapers, medical supplies and a sleeping basket to put next to our bed—the minimum equipment to bring a baby home. We hadn't taken much for granted, as if it would have brought bad luck to presume.

I felt battered. Even my ribs, arms and neck were sore. I kept looking out the window, feeling sorry for myself. I didn't want to talk to anyone. Planning for uncertainty didn't give any comfort now. I should have made a perfect nursery. Then I could have sat in the rocking chair, surveying a row of silly-faced, terry cloth animals and a stack of freshly washed blankets, and I could have cried and cried for my losses. If the baby died, people could say, Can you imagine, she had to pack away all the little clothes. But in our cautious household, the clothes were still packed.

Fred called the nursery, identifying himself as the father of Cade. How strange that sounded. I was the mother of Cade. Across the park and over the hill, we had a baby. The nurse gave the phone to a doctor, who told Fred that they were hyperventilating the baby now, in an effort to improve her oxygenation. She was receiving 120 breaths a minute. She seemed stable for the moment. We imagined her chest fluttering up and down. The triangle of skin under the center of her ribs would rise and deflate, too quickly to count at that breath rate, alterable with the turn of a dial, as if our baby were merely an extension of a machine. Later, I slept on my back, which I hadn't done for months, since that position can reduce the flow of oxygen to the baby.

At 6 a.m. on Thursday, Cade was almost a day and a half old. I called the intensive care nursery, and the nurse said that she had experienced a "circular night." She had improved but then worsened, and was "in crisis" between 3 and 4:30 a.m. Two doctors were working on her now. We would have to wait and see. "OK," I said. "Thank you. We'll come in." I told Fred what she'd said. We didn't like to panic. We'd felt—having made phone calls, dealt with the breastpump, rented a car, talked to doctors and understood them, read the ICN orientation packet—we'd felt that we could handle the business of the day. Take it as it comes. But a crisis happened while we were sleeping, not with her, and we didn't even know what had happened. I was desperate for words. What did "in crisis" mean? I'd read a shelf's worth of pregnancy books, but there was no book for us now, no translation of hospital language. What were the two doctors doing right now? The nurse had seemed to speak reluctantly, uncertainly. Why was I sleeping in my bed while my baby was suffering? Fred enclosed me in his arms so I couldn't see anything, and I cried hard against him. Then we dressed in the clothes we'd thrown on the floor the night before and drove to the hospital.

The nurse was writing on a clipboard. Fred fastened his gown as he walked quickly into the nursery. "How is she?"

"Holding on." She smiled sympathetically. "She had a bad time there."

"Two doctors were working on her?" I asked. The ICN seemed tranquil now, as if nothing had happened. No doctors were present. Cade looked the same as when we'd left the night before—body stilled, eyes closed, head turned to one side, tube in her mouth.

"They worked to improve her oxygen saturation." She pointed to the monitor at the foot of the bed, where blue numbers glowed against a black screen, showing a "sat" rate, or rate of oxygen saturation. They were giving her 100 percent oxygen, but her body was not absorbing that much. Her body was only oxygenating blood at a minimal rate. The sat number was the rate, and represented an estimate. The real rate was obtained by taking blood via her umbilical catheter and testing it in the lab for oxygen. The nurse's explanation made sense, but I still didn't know what the doctors had done. We only learned much later from reading medical records that they had taken the baby off the ventilator temporarily and manually resuscitated her. They had discontinued the paralyzing Pavulon and the morphine to prevent respiratory failure, then cautiously restarted them at 5:30 a.m.

It disturbed me that no one had called us when Cade was in crisis. I didn't want to answer the phone at home and hear someone tell me, Your baby died; I wanted someone to call before that. But we didn't want to make a fuss now, figuring we'd save any unpleasantness for important matters. In the midst of an emergency, who had time to telephone the parents? We were peripheral; if doctors were working on her, we wouldn't even be allowed in the nursery. Still, I'd rather have been at the hospital than sleeping at home. A formal act of panicking might have been as therapeutic as a formal act of grieving, the equivalent of a funeral. We could have paced the halls all night, waiting for someone to emerge and give us news. If she were going, it would help us to hold her hand and say goodbye before she left us. Now we could only sit on our stools in numbness, behaving reasonably, asking logical questions in the daylit room.

Dr. Hanover stepped in and leaned back against the sink, his arms crossed.

"She had a difficult night," I said.

"Yup."

Fred tried. "Do you think she's improving?"

He scratched an eyebrow. "Early to say."

"For the blood gas," I said. "What are good numbers?"

"A lot of parents focus on the numbers," he said. "When they really shouldn't. There's no absolute good number to look for."

What else did we have to focus on? If a lot of parents focused on the numbers, then surely it was out of a natural need. Cade's mouth hung open, her lower lip free of tape; the bottom of her mouth looked as if she'd fallen asleep sitting up. Her top lip and the space between her mouth and nose were plastered with translucent white tape, which held the respirator tube in place. Her chest fluttered up and down. Her face looked puffier, the bags under her eyes yellower. Hanover said she might have a little jaundice, nothing to worry about, and that she was eliminating fluids fairly well.

"Her kidneys work," he said. "That's good."

I hadn't considered that her kidneys might not work. What else were they worrying about?

The nurse asked us to leave so they could check the baby's breathing tube. We wandered the halls, not knowing that her oxygen index was approaching 40, a number that indicated an 80 percent chance of mortality and warranted the lung bypass machine, or ECMO. As they had done at 3:30 a.m., Jim Spicer, the respiratory therapist on duty, and another therapist were disconnecting the ventilator and manually pumping air into her for a minute with a green rubber balloon to find a rate and pressure at which her lungs would absorb oxygen. The resident examined Cade, advising that the pressure and breath rate should be lowered that day, to avoid life-threatening lung injury. When she'd finished, the therapists hand-bagged for three minutes, then reconnected the baby to the ventilator. We came back in briefly before rounds, the two-hour period when we couldn't be in the nursery; the medical team would assemble before each baby and consider its case. The rounds summary sheet for Cade read simply, "Too sick to discuss."

By late afternoon on Thursday, Cade had not stabilized. She was receiving double-strength dopamine at the maximum dose, to raise her blood pressure. The monitors beeped often, when her pressure or oxygen saturation dipped too low, and Hanover stayed in the nursery, leaning against the sink. Fred and I sat on cushioned stools pulled up to her table. The stools were awkwardly high, like barstools with backs, and stuck out in the small space. Dr. Hanover stood only two feet behind us. Fred turned on his stool. "What's the thinking on ECMO now?"

"We're watching her numbers," Hanover said. "It's a definite possibility." We all stayed silent for a while.

"Is ECMO always the last resort?" I said.

"Depends." He scratched his beard. "The machine allows the lungs to rest and possibly heal." As we learned later, putting a baby on the lung bypass machine involved inserting a tube into the right carotid artery to drain blood from the right atrium of the heart, running the blood through an oxygenation process, and returning it to the body via the jugular vein.

"So whether you use it depends on what," I said.

"It may not be appropriate, if we're dealing with advanced pneumonitis, for instance."

"Then you wouldn't use the ECMO?" Fred said.

"Antibiotics might be more efficacious." He waved his hand. "No sense talking about hypotheticals."

I'd been focusing on the lung bypass machine, thinking that if she were going to die, they'd put her on that first. We could feel safe because they'd tell us she needed the ECMO; it was a barrier before death. She wouldn't just die at any minute on her warming table. If she didn't stabilize, we would be discussing the risks of transport, familiarizing ourselves with the intensive care nursery at the better-equipped University of California at San Francisco Hospital, keeping our vigil over Cade and her new machine. Obviously there were scenarios I hadn't conceived of. We'd been told Cade might die, and although I'd considered the impact of that idea, I didn't imagine the physical process of my baby dying, her dead body, wouldn't cast that blue shadow over her like a smothering wing. She lay bathed in the perpetual white-gold light of warming lamps, the nursery dim around her. We all watched her chest beating, 74 times a minute now. I shifted my weight. Hanover asked, "Are you getting some rest?"

"Yes."

"You need rest now," he said, with grandfatherly kindness. I flushed at this unexpected attention and turned back to the baby, distracted. Beyond her table surrounded by equipment was a clear plastic isolette with a tiny infant inside, Baby Ashley. Baby Ashley's mother was sitting on a stool, her yellow-gowned arms stuck through two portholes to change her baby. I thought her clothes were tacky: a bright, jungle-print blouse with stretch jeans and new, white, aerobic sneakers. She wore pastel-colored eyeshadow, blusher and lipstick, and her long brown hair was permed into crinkles. The yellow sterile gown looked almost as ugly on her as it did on me.

I wondered why Cade wasn't in an isolette, like Ashley. Maybe only preemies lived in them, being too fragile to come outside. When Hanover ducked out for a minute, I asked the nurse why Cade was on a table. So they could get to her quickly if they had to, she explained. And the warming lights regulated her body temperature better than an incubator, whose portholes allowed the air inside to heat and cool.

I'd taken her being on this table as a good sign, evidence that she was more robust than other babies. My assumptions were being corrected too often, and I began to feel out of kilter. I remembered when my sister tripped and fell flat as a child, cracking her cheekbone on the neighbor's brick terrace. Two doctors had questioned me separately and I'd realized—oh!—that they thought someone had hit her. And I recalled finding my grandmother's lovely white teeth in a motel-room glass. Recent love letters from a high school girl in the underwear drawer of a man I lived with. These moments occurred years apart, so I didn't have to feel bewildered; I could still be at home in the world. In this hospital, I was making too many mistakes. How could I get better at knowing what the hell was going on?

The nursery consisted of three rooms in a row, with dividing walls of glass from waist level up, and open doorways between rooms. We were in the first room on the left. I could see only into the middle room, which held three babies in incubators. So Cade was the only baby on a warming bed. Was she the sickest one, sicker than the red-skinned babies half her size? I couldn't believe those tiny, sick-looking babies had a better chance than she did. When Hanover came back in, I said quietly, "So I just want to know, it's very possible she may not make it." I knew he thought that was an unnecessary question. Fred probably thought it was a stupid question, which it was. Both of them looked for a long moment at me, the dull one who needed everything spelled out.

Hanover said, "She might not."

Outside the nursery, I told Fred we should tell our parents they could come and see her. I felt panicked with guilt over my mother. She wanted to come, and I'd kept her away. My mother and I were extremely close, but Fred and my mother still had a certain distance between them. I'd hesitated to have my mother come help with the baby, fearing that Fred might be pushed aside. When Cade was ill, I felt even more strongly that Fred and I needed to lock together and that we couldn't afford to have him feel left out. But it was my mother's first grandchild, the first grandchild on my side of the family. Cade might die, and my mother wouldn't have seen her. I insisted that we call all of the grandparents.

I began to believe, too, that if Cade died unseen, it would be only Fred's and my loss. She wouldn't seem real to anyone else. And maybe if Cade died I could forget her, too. I needed a collective memory to give mine authority. Fred and I had sat up in bed and decided that if she died we would take a long trip to Indonesia. Her death would be a terrible episode in our lives that we would recover from; maybe we would have no children, then, and become minor tragic figures, expatriate writers with a dead baby. There was a self-important glamour in that, an allure to the idea of drinking ourselves into oblivion on a beach somewhere. We would survive our child's death, more or less. But we were here. The baby was still alive.

My mother wasn't home, and I didn't want to leave an unsettling message. Fred reached his mother. He said, "Hi. She's not doing so great. We thought—"Then he started to cry, the only time I saw him cry during this, and he blindly pushed the phone at me. I explained that we didn't want people coming out for us, but that if they wanted to see Cade, they should feel free to come. I really couldn't bear the thought of people snuffling and hugging me, talking about me in lowered voices while I lay resting in the afternoon, the bedroom blinds pulled down. Stiff and stoical was my preferred posture. Carol was matter-of-fact, as always, so it was possible for me to remain composed. She had been pragmatic when her husband lay near death for several months in a Milwaukee hospital. She researched his heart condition and all the surgeries and questioned the specialists who worked on him. She knew his treatments and several times had to correct the nurses when they gave him the wrong kind or amount of medication. She was tough. I liked talking to her.

When I called my father, my stepmother answered; he wasn't home. It was 8 p.m. on the East Coast, and she'd had a few drinks, which wasn't unusual for that time of night. I liked to call them on Saturday afternoons, after my father had played tennis, before the cocktail hour. I made my statement, and rolled my eyes at Fred as she started asking questions. This wasn't about my father, she said, this was about me, wasn't it? I needed him to come. He didn't need to come. What would she tell my father when he got home, I wondered. She persisted—wasn't this really about me? What did I need? Yes, the request was for me, but it was also for him, I tried to explain. If my dad didn't get the chance to meet his first grandchild, he might feel sorry. I hated her booze-slowed psychologizing, as if anyone had time to figure it all out just then.

Dr. Hanover wrote notes in Cade's chart at 6 p.m. Thursday. The baby had been alive for almost two days. He must have been tired. "Have been in attendance since 0800," he began. His notes, usually in almost-fluid prose, were cryptic scrawls. "Paralyzed," he wrote, and "Persistent fetal circulation—severe." Oxygenation was difficult.

"Will prob need TX in next 1-2 d," he wrote, indicating the need for a blood transfusion. He described us as "in to visit/touch for long intervals." The equation of visit and touch is telling—he always wanted us to touch her, even as alarms went off and nurses glared at us for disturbing her. He believed in the laying on of hands. We were aware of our baby's "grave condition, without much room to spare should oxygenation decrease—also aware of possibility of transfer to ECMO if condition worsens." He wrote sideways in the margin, maybe to add a hopeful note, "Lung fluids much clearer!"

In the ICN, we were learning more from the nurses, some of whom explained numbers and monitors to us. Cade had many different nurses during her stay, and we often felt disconcerted to walk in and see an unfamiliar one. That night a new nurse taught us about pH and PaCO2, the measurements of acidity and carbon dioxide in Cade's blood. Blood gas tests revealed these numbers, which we remembered watching for Fred's father. When the numbers came within a certain range, the blood vessels in the lungs might dilate again and allow blood to pass through. Now, the ventilator forced air into her lungs, and the longer she was on the ventilator—especially with high concentrations of oxygen, which damaged lung tissue—the higher the risk became that the ventilator would blow a hole in her lung. A hole in the lung, the nurse explained, could be fatal if it happened outside a hospital. You stop breathing, and surgery is required immediately. If Cade had a hole, it would set her back, but it probably wouldn't cause her to die.

How harsh all of the treatment was on her body—the ventilator, the toxic oxygen, the Pavulon that paralyzed her, the morphine. Her whole body appeared yellowish to me, especially where fluid had accumulated to form bags under her closed eyes. Her hair, never washed or brushed, matted darkly on her scalp. An IV had been moved to the top of her head, and, out of a mass of tape plastered at all angles, the needle stuck up at a tilt.

"Good veins up there," the nurse commented. "Have you thought about a music box? Some parents bring in a tape player or music box."

"We'll get one," Fred said. "Today." He looked as stricken as I felt—we hadn't thought of it. Baby Ashley's isolette was decorated with puffy stuffed animals and pictures taped to the sides. Every time we left Cade we felt as if we were abandoning her, and we'd been leaving nothing of ourselves behind. Toys and pictures seemed absurd—she couldn't move, her eyes were closed. Yet if these things could possibly help, she should have them. I wondered what else ICN parents did that we had overlooked.

The nurse invited us to stay while she did a blood gas, which made us feel welcome, as if we belonged there. She untwisted a plastic cap from the end of the skinny tube coming from Cade's umbilicus and screwed on a syringe. Bright blood came up into the curling tube, looped a loop, and flooded the small chamber of the syringe. She detached the syringe and laid it on a tray, recapped the tube, shook the syringe, dropped it in a plastic bag which she sealed and labeled, placed it on a bed of ice in a plastic tub, and carried it to the dumbwaiter in the next room. She called the lab to say it was coming. The results would be sent in half an hour.

In the closed snack bar, Fred unstacked two chairs and pulled them up to a table. We lifted food out of a bag our friend Alan had brought and exclaimed over it: fried chicken, green salad, a round loaf of bread, cookies, mineral water, an egg-sized chocolate truffle in a shiny white box. We ate everything with our hands, by light that slanted in from the hall, hardly speaking because we were hungry. We laughed over the image of Alan standing in front of the deli counter at a grocery store, ordering chicken and wildly picking up everything else he saw around him.

When we returned to the ICN, Cade seemed more stable than the night before; the lab tests indicated no change. Her blood pressure had improved, and her dopamine dosage had been reduced. "Maybe she's turning the corner." The nurse tilted her head, inviting us to agree.

"Hmmm," Fred said, and I said, "Good," but we didn't let ourselves believe her.

I called my mother from a hospital pay phone, anxious to reach her, since I'd already told the other grandparents they could come. She said she'd get there as soon as she could, probably Saturday.

"Cade is going to make it," she said. "I just know it. She's 7 pounds, so strong!"

"But Mom," I said, annoyed. "Only full-term babies suffer from meconium aspiration. The smaller ones can't have a bowel movement." Meconium, a thick, tarry substance, is an infant's first excretion, sometimes in utero. Babies can swallow small amounts of it before delivery, which isn't serious, and can inhale what's in their mouths after the umbilical cord is cut, which is what happened to Cade.

"I still think she'll be fine," she said. "She's got good genes." I gave her a loud sigh. She would obviously say whatever illogical thing she could think of to convince me. I didn't want to be convinced that the baby would live, demanding instead that my mother accept reality and listen to me. I wavered from serenity to fretfulness to despair.

I complained about Dr. Hanover's unwillingness to tell us much. He acted evasive, defensive, condescending. What if he were defensive because he didn't know what he was doing? How could we find out about his professional reputation? Mom said she would make some calls in the morning and learn what she could; if he wasn't a good doctor, we would find another one.

I didn't think in large amounts of time, then. I thought in minutes, in hours. When I was pregnant I could think in years, of putting a child on the schoolbus, of walking in the woods and collecting leaves to press in a book. I used to have a leaf-pressing kit. "Having a child will bring out the best in us," I'd said to Fred. We'd be curious again, we'd invent rituals to mark the seasons, we'd rent a cabin some summer and teach ourselves to fish. Now time had shrunk. I felt shut down, alert only to physical sensation, facts and numbers. Was it shock, or fear, or a practiced autopilot?

I'm sure some of my stubborn inhabitance of the moment came from practice in childbirth class of focusing on the present contraction, the present pain, and not panicking about the 50 increasingly painful contractions yet to come. This was added to years of practice at staying relatively serene, after having been diagnosed with manic depression: I was hospitalized at a psychiatric facility in November of my senior year in high school. I was on an open ward, with other suicidal types, heavily drugged schizophrenics and a couple of incorrigible alcoholics. The ward felt safer than my high school culture, which crackled with sex and heavy drinking around a nucleus of academic work. The academic work was fine, except for my certainty that no good college would accept me. My parents drove me for college tours and interviews from Duke in the South to Wesleyan in the Northeast, and all the while I felt like a tainted specimen, too small, too shy, too unathletic. My private high school was full of healthy children of the rich, who played soccer and lacrosse and vacationed at Aspen; they'd frightened me when I'd first seen them as eighth-graders, in their bright madras clothes and silver braces. Now I am curious about them, in their adult forms as New York City stockbrokers and interior decorators. With their stone houses in New Jersey, their Scotch, their extramarital affairs, their antique furniture, golden retrievers—they've become the parents of children I knew, the parents who scrutinized me, an outsider, as the most likely conduit to anything nasty their children might be indulging in. Their children had already secured a place in the world. Who was I?

Boys liked me for a girlfriend, and so I got invited in. The story of the next years doesn't belong; I hope it is enough to say that while I made friends I still have today, and worked hard for inspiring teachers, I also engaged in an excessive social life and became repetitively, but not terminally, self-destructive. One day, I met for one hour with a psychiatrist and was committed to the hospital for observation. (My mother must have been relieved; having a daughter who swallows all of the Tylenol in the house and then calls you at work to tell you so is surely no fun.) And it was fine there, with many amusements—making leather bracelets, writing poems about feelings, doing jumping jacks in the gym with people on Thorazine who couldn't even clap their hands together. When I left on a day pass to watch a soccer game at school, I couldn't wait to get back to the hospital, where everyone felt uncomfortable with themselves. And yet I wouldn't ever want to do it again. I was still a child at the time, and my failures could be covered up by my school headmaster, who attested in my college file that I had missed school due to pneumonia. My weaknesses could be addressed by my mother, who wouldn't leave me alone. I slept for a while in the bedroom next to hers, a warm, narrow room filled with her old, sustaining books by Virginia Woolf and Doris Lessing.

My discharge diagnosis was manic depression. Lithium had no effect on me, but the clinic psychiatrist told me I'd not live a normal life without medication, and he prescribed antidepressants. The doctor was wrong, of course—my medicated life lasted only two months. It ended when I despairingly swallowed a whole bottle of antidepressants (with minimal effort since they looked exactly like tiny, spicy red-hot candies) soon after my boyfriend told me he had a crush on someone else at school.

I distrusted my hospital doctors, who could label me so peremptorily and absolutely as manic-depressive. And while their diagnosis felt wrong, I also distrusted myself, knowing that every feeling of euphoria would be followed by a crash, knowing, over the years, that Plath and Woolf didn't commit suicide because of a new, especially profound depression, but because of the sheer tedium of repetitive suicidal desire. It's happening again, I would think bitterly, as I sat in my apartment in one city or another, unable to pick up the telephone or eat or take a shower or vacuum or change my clothes. So during the in-between times, which gradually have stretched farther and farther, I'd always think: even keel. Keep the keel in the water. I pictured a white sailboat keel in cold greenish water, the brine of Nova Scotia of an Elizabeth Bishop poem, or of Maine where my dad took us sailing. If we didn't keep the proper balance on the boat, it would heel to the side, and the keel, the long, planar sharkfin of it, would threaten to whoosh to the surface as we all got dumped overboard. Falling into water is fine. But falling toward the extremes of what's now labeled bipolar illness is not. So I'd tell myself, Don't scream, don't shout with joy, don't drink too much. Much happiness has come to me this way. If you think this willful numbing of emotion is wrong or sad, please don't. I still drink a glass of wine, sing when my friend plays the guitar, and love my husband; I just don't drink the whole bottle, sleep with strangers, or regard razorblades as instruments of release from a shameful life. Sometimes emotions, as fashionable as they are, don't help me. When my baby was in the hospital, I often retreated to a more primary source of being: my body. What did I see, hear and touch, and what did it mean? Isn't this how infants learn the world?

That night, while we slept, the baby opened her eyes in the nursery. The overhead warming lamps must have been very bright for her. She was immediately given Pavulon and morphine, and within 30 seconds, she closed her eyes again.

My father woke us by 7 a.m. Friday morning to say that he'd be arriving in San Francisco in the evening. I was stunned. Except for our visits to him near Christmas, he had governed as a father from afar, ensconced in a comfortable house with his wife and stepdaughter. Our relationship was almost not a relationship, though he had been warmer and more attentive during my pregnancy. He and Maureen had visited while I was confined to bed in June. They sat uncomfortably in our garage-sale chairs. We discussed their trip and the weather. I'd accepted that my father and I, who looked alike and were both stonily stubborn, had already passed our best years together. When I was a child I knew he loved me, knowledge that could last my whole life, even if he didn't like me much anymore. But he'd made efforts during the visit, reading the paper and watching tennis on television, buying me a 50-foot telephone cord, bringing in take-out food. He seemed to be taking his grandfather's role quite seriously. I failed to give Maureen any credit: As I discovered later, it was Maureen who had insisted they come to the hospital right away, buying airline tickets as my father mentally reviewed his work calendar for a less-busy day.

When we arrived at the hospital, as became our habit, one of us rushed in to see Cade while the other deposited chilled breastmilk in the nursery freezer and piled our jackets and bags in a parents' room. I hurried to the nursery first, and Dr. Hanover stopped me in the anteroom. "People are calling me from Washington," he said evenly. "I can't give out details of this case; it's confidential information." He slapped down a manila folder on the desk. "You know that."

I didn't step backwards, though I wanted to. "I'm sorry."

"Who do you want me to talk to? Why don't you ask me what you want to know?" He was getting more and more nettled. "Who is in Washington?" he said loudly, and the unit assistant looked up at him. "I've got the head of hospital calling me and asking to be briefed on this case. Who is ordering these telephone calls?"

"My mother is in Washington," I said. "I asked her to get some information."

"I will be glad," he sniffed, thoroughly put out, "to speak with her personally after rounds."

"Thank you." I turned away from him to wash my hands, and he picked up his file and opened it.

At home during rounds, I called my sister, who was in Washington visiting our mother before graduate film school started again in Los Angeles. I had to talk to her, but I didn't want to; I was too tired. With Mom I talked facts, with Cecily interpretation, and I couldn't articulate my feelings yet. When she'd been ill earlier in the summer, she'd gone to the hospital over and over for invasive tests with disturbing results, and I couldn't really feel what that was like, I could only wish she didn't have to feel it. How could she feel what this was like for me? I didn't even know what this was like for me, or what it even was. A terrible thing was happening to me, and yet it wasn't happening to me, it was happening to my baby. "I'm so tired," I said.

"I know," she said. "Mom keeps saying the baby will be fine."

"Nobody knows if the baby will be fine," I said vehemently.

"She's driving me crazy."

I laughed. "Is she clicking her nails on her coffee cup?" Our mother always signaled us when we'd lingered too long at breakfast and should be getting out and about.

"She'll hardly sit down."

"Poor Mom."

"I know," Cecily sighed. "So you're going back and forth to the hospital?"

"All day. We're in a routine."

"You're busy."

"It's good. We have very little time to think." It was odd that she happened to be at our mother's house instead of her apartment in Los Angeles; I felt flung back in time to when she was in high school and I'd left for college. I'd call in with all my big news from the world, like how many slides we had to memorize for the art history exam, or what I'd done on Saturday night. "I do icepacks and sitz baths, and there's breastpumping. Fred sterilizes the pump every morning."

"I am never having a baby," she said firmly.

As we talked, our mother was at work, waiting in a hallway of the Senate Office Building for a hearing to finish. She called the HMO representative in Washington again, who told her that he'd heard the situation was critical, and the baby might not live. If it were him, he said, he'd get on a plane for California. Yes, she told him, she'd already reserved the first seat available. When she recounted this conversation to me months later, I was surprised that she'd known how ill Cade was. I thought she didn't realize it, that she wasn't listening to me. I was also startled that the hospital's official word had been that the baby might not live. The doctors and nurses and respiratory therapists went about their work calmly, of course, since critical illness was routine for them in this nursery. They never brought up death, and I'd begun to feel as if I were extreme or hysterical to focus on the possibility. In the ICN, we seemed to exist in a futureless present tense, in which we could discuss medications and strategies, but never a prognosis.

After rounds, Baby Ashley's mother sat on a stool beyond Cade's table, her back to Ashley's isolette. Dr. Hanover faced her from a low chair. We usually minded our own business in the nursery, not wandering around to look at other babies, not listening too closely to the nurses discussing cases, or weekend plans, not often meeting the eyes of other parents as they came and went. We acted the same way everyone did. All of the families seemed to crave privacy, to create an invisible perimeter around their baby's area, bounded by respirators, IV carts and a nurse in a chair. But we could not help overhearing Baby Ashley's mother say, "Part of her brain is missing?"

"The tests seem to indicate," Hanover said, and we couldn't hear the rest.

The mother straightened up on her stool; she looked pinned to it. "Which part?"

"It's not a very important part," Hanover said affably. "It's the kind of lack you can make up for by reading her lots of books, that sort of thing." I saw her struggling to formulate questions, and I knew her struggle. Hanover would give a morsel of information, and I would think, What is the question? What is the question I can ask that will elicit more information? If I don't ask a precise question, he won't tell me anything. She asked something about the cerebral cortex. I knew those words, but only as I heard her say them; I couldn't have summoned them up and asked that question. Where was her husband, and why did Hanover look as relaxed as if he were discussing the Sunday paper? Read her lots of books. I was ashamed to have thought of Ashley's mother as tacky. She persisted with questions while the doctor looked blandly back at her.

My mother was silent when I called from home to tell her Dad was coming that night. She would come the next night, Saturday, and leave Monday morning. Grandparents' visiting hours were from 1-2 p.m. and 7-8 p.m. every day. One grandparent could be in the room with one parent. It made me tense to think about portioning out the time between my father, his wife and my mother.

My mother said, "The director has asked around about Dr. Hanover, and the word is, he has an excellent reputation."

"Really?"

"Critically ill babies from other Bay Area hospitals are often sent to him."

This news gave me tremendous hope. If he could save babies that other hospitals couldn't handle, then Cade was getting the best possible care. "Who cares if the man won't talk?" I said lightly.

"Exactly," my mother said. "As long as he saves our baby."

We rushed back to the hospital to be there at 7:24 p.m. Cade would be 3 days old, and Fred had decided that we should be with her at her birth time every day; I had only just caught on. We quickly scrubbed and gowned and pulled up two high stools to her table, one of us on each side. I sat between her table and the door, pulled up close so people could walk behind me. On the other side of the table, Fred sat with his stool carefully placed among a nest of wires. To his right was the ventilator, a blue box on a stand, with digital readouts of breaths being given per minute, percentage of pure oxygen and something called "PEEP." The blood pressure and heart rate monitor hung over Fred's left shoulder. On the wall, the pink-and-white "I'm a Girl" card with Cade's birth information now had "Dad - Fred" written on it. We softly touched Cade's arms and said, as we always did, "Hi honey, it's Mom and Dad. We're here." We told her she'd made it through three whole days, and how brave she was, and that grandparents were coming to see her the next day. Her head was turned so she was facing Fred. We took out the things we'd brought for her: a photograph of the two of us that my mother had taken at Christmas, when I was nine weeks pregnant, in which Fred has his arms around me, and we are leaning back in a restaurant banquette, looking happy; a black-and-white terrycloth puppy with a red bow around its neck, chosen because the nurse said babies see only contrast, not colors, at first; and a wind-up music box. We taped the photo to the clear plastic barrier she faced and placed the puppy below it. We put the music box out of the way at a bottom corner of the bed. I felt much better having brought these tokens, as if they would give her comfort, as if we could bring pieces of home to her.

The intensive care nursery couldn't have been less like home, with its sterile paper gowns, electronic sounds, equipment housed in metal boxes. Yet it was a human place. Ashley's nurse shook out her blond hair and talked with Ashley's mom about aerobics class; another nurse called his little girl at home to say goodnight. While Fred and I stared at Cade as if willing her to wake up—though medicine, not sleep, kept her eyes closed—we listened to the almost inaudible sound of a country-western song being played at low volume in the anteroom, the unit assistant tapping time with his pencil on the desk.

Kathryn Rhett *is an assistant professor at Gettysburg College. Her poems have been published in* The Antioch Review, Ploughshares *and elsewhere. She just recently edited an anthology entitled "Survival Stories: Memoirs of Crisis," (Doubleday) which is due out in August. This essay has been excerpted from her new book, "Near Breathing," published by Duquesne University Press as part of the Emerging Writers in Creative Nonfiction book series.*

An Album Quilt

John McPhee

*T*hat August I returned to the town in New Jersey where I had been born 50 years before. It looked much the same. Any town would, after five weeks.

There was a great deal of waiting mail—08540, 08540, 08540. Not for nothing does that begin and end with a zero, I reflected. Good to be home. Nice to lift up the edges and crawl in under the only zip code I've ever known. A zip that doesn't flap. A zip that can be tied down. A zip with grommets at either end.

I opened a letter from a staff writer at a national travel magazine compiled and edited in Tennessee.

"I would appreciate it very much if you could answer some questions I have about New Jersey ... I would like to know why a writer, who could live almost anywhere he wanted to, chooses to live in New Jersey."

Is he kidding? I have just come home from Alaska, from a long drift on the Yukon River, where, virtually under doctor's orders, I must go from time to time to recover from the sheer physiographic intensity of living in New Jersey—must go, to be reminded that there is at least one other state that is physically as varied but is sensibly spread out. New Jersey was bisected in 1664, when a boundary line was drawn from Little Egg Harbor to the Delaware River near the Water Gap so that this earth of majesty, this fortress built by Nature for herself, could be deeded by the Duke of York to Lord Berkeley and George Carteret. If you travel that line—the surveyors' pylons still stand—you traverse the physiographic provinces of New Jersey. You cross the Coastal Plain. You cross the Triassic Lowlands, a successor basin. You cross the Blue Ridge, crystalline hills. Now before you is the centerpiece of a limestone valley that runs south from New Jersey to Alabama and north from New Jersey into Canada—one valley, known to science as the Great Valley of the Appalachians and to local peoples here and there as Champlain, Shenandoah, Clinch River Valley, but in New Jersey by no special name, for in terrain so cornucopian one does not tend to notice a Shenandoah. A limestone valley is a white silo, a white barn, a sweep of ground so beautiful it should never end. You cross the broad valley. You rise now into the folded and faulted mountains, the eastern sinuous welt, the Deformed Appalachians themselves. You are still in New Jersey.

Are they aware of this in Tennessee? When you cross New Jersey, you cover four events: the violent upheaval of two sets of mountains several hundred million years apart; and, long after all that, the creation of the Atlantic Ocean; and, more recently, the laying on of the Coastal Plain by the trowel of the Mason. Do they know that in Tennessee? Tennessee is a one-event country: All you see there, east to west, are the Appalachians, slowly going away.

New Jersey has had the genius to build across its narrow center the most concentrated transportation slot in the world—with three or four railroads, seaports, highways and an international airport all compacted in effect into a tube, a conduit, which has acquired through time an ugliness sufficient to stop a Gorgon in her tracks. Through this supersluice continuously pass hundreds of thousands of people from Nebraska, Kansas, Illinois, Iowa, Texas, Tennessee, holding their breath. They are shot like peas to New York. If New Jersey has a secret, that is it.

I remember Fred Brown, who lived in the Pine Barrens of the New Jersey Coastal Plain, remarking years ago outside his shanty, "I never been nowheres where I liked it better than I do here. I like to walk where you can walk on level ground. Outside here, if I stand still, 15 or 20 quail, couple of coveys, will come out and go around. The gray fox don't come in no nearer than the swamp there, but I've had the coons come in here, the deer will come up. Muskrats breed right here, and otters sometimes. I was to Tennessee once. They're greedy, hungry, there, to Tennessee. They'll pretty near take the back off your hand when you lay down money. I never been nowhere I liked better than here."

It has somehow become 1978 and for 10 or 15 years I have been intending to attempt a piece of writing called "Six Princetons"—the school as it has variously appeared to someone who was born in Princeton and has lived in Princeton all his life. It would begin with the little kid who knew the location of every pool table and Hajoca urinal on the campus, the nine best ways to sneak into the gym, the gentlest method of removing a reunion costume from a sleeping drunk. Princeton through the eyes of a student in Princeton High School. Princeton from the 20-20 omnicomprehensive undergraduate perspective. Princeton from the point of view of a commuter absorbed with other worlds. (Once, in that era, I found myself saying to my wife, "What are all these young people doing on Nassau Street?") The Princeton University library and campus studied from across the street by an incarcerated freelance who stares out an upstairs office window all through the day. (My next-door neighbor is the Swedish Massage Studio, a legitimate business which darkens at 5 p.m. Later in the evening, the Swedish Massage's unwanted customers see my light and come tapping on my door. When I open up, their faces fall. "Is this the Swedish Massage?" they say incredulously, their disappointment all too apparent at the sight of the hoar in the beard.) Princeton a fixed foot, as it appears after long stays elsewhere. Princeton as witnessed by a perennial, paradoxical "visiting professor" who is neither visiting nor a professor, but in spring semester after spring semester is given tonic by a roomful of writing students who yield as much as they receive.

"Six Princetons" will never be written, though, because new Princetons keep coming along. "Dear Parent: We are pleased to inform you that your daughter has succeeded you as an editor of the Nassau Literary Review, and, incidentally, that her room-board-tuition for the academic year 1978-79 has been raised *quinque per centum* to $2,500,000."

As I write this, in 1983, one of my daughters is somewhere in India, another is believed to be in Egypt, another is skating on a north Italian pond, and the oldest is working as a writer in Pittstown, New Jersey. There is a moral in this tale.

My children have always thought me mildly eccentric for living my whole life in one town, yet there is no need to move away from Princeton to get a change of scene. You stay here all your life and you get a new town every five years.

When you are young and getting married, or your daughter is getting married and your own youth is silt in the river, you turn to Nature for instruction and example. And so Laura and I, one truly fine day, went a couple of hundred kilometers into Iceland's interior for the ritual purpose of consulting Nature to see what we might learn.

Along the way we stopped at Geysir, where a great hole in the ground is the world's eponymous geyser. The old geyser is no longer forthcoming. It is full of water but not of action. It had literally been roped off. Close at hand was a young geyser. At five- to seven-minute intervals—no more than that—it swelled tumescently, let forth a series of heavy grunts, and into the sky shot a plume of flying steam. Meanwhile, the old geyser just sat there—boiling. We learned how—on special occasions—Icelanders make the old geyser do its thing. They throw soap into it, and it erupts.

Moving on, we passed a waterfall of the size of the American Niagara, and then we drove for an hour or two on the gravels of an outwash plain that was covered with rounded boulders and no vegetation, not so much as a clump of grass. Eventually, the car could go no farther, so we left it behind and proceeded north on foot. There was a stream to ford. Laura had running shoes, and I had boots. She got onto my back, and I carried her across. We then walked a couple of miles, also on rounded rocks, and up onto a high moraine, where, coming over the crest, we looked down into a lake back-dropped by cliffs of blue ice. This was the edge not of a valley glacier but of an ice cap covering nearly 500 square miles. Above the lake, the ice wall rose about 150 feet, and was sheer. There came sounds like high-powered-rifle shots, as huge bergs calved away from the ice cap and plunged into the water. There was no going farther. On the way down the moraine and back toward the river ford, I attempted to increase my credit line by mentioning that glacial rivers grow in the afternoon with the day's melt from the sun, and this time we could expect a larger river when I carried her across it. But this time she was having none of me. Apparently, she had forded her last river on her father's back. She took off her shoes and negotiated the stream.

My admired and beloved son-in-law is a professional writer. A professional writer, by definition, is a person clothed in self-denial who each and almost every day will plead with eloquent lamentation that he has a brutal burden on his mind and soul, will summon deep reserves of "discipline" as seriatim antidotes to any domestic chore, and, drawing the long sad face of the pale poet, will rise above his dread of his dreaded working chamber, excuse himself from the idle crowd, go into his writing sanctum, shut the door, shoot the bolt, and in lonely sacrifice turn on the tube and watch the Mets game.

Idaho Springs, Colorado, dawn. A white rented car. Alone, I toss my gear into the trunk and get going early. After a couple of miles, I note in the rear-view mirror that the back window is fogged over. "Condensation," I tell myself. "Car dew. It will soon evaporate." I get up onto Interstate 70 and head west. Now and again, I look in the mirror. Visibility zero. Evaporation has not yet kicked in. Twenty miles. Twenty-five. Climbing. Eventually, I realize that when I put my gear in the trunk I did not close the lid. I don't know whatever else I was once. Now I'm a little, gray-bearded, absent-minded professor. With events like this one in mind, my daughter Jenny has long called me Lefty. I don't think I'm going to recover. I don't think I'm going to go backwards.

In the late 1970s and early 1980s, I collected material in Wyoming for a book about the geology there. Almost without exception, those journeys were made in the company of John David Love, of the United States Geological Survey, who had started life in 1913 on a solitary ranch in the center of the state and had long since achieved a reputation of preeminence among Rocky Mountain geologists. My intention was to try to present the natural history of his region through his eyes and his experience. It is not uncommon for a geologist to reflect in the style of his science the structure of his home terrain.

We had been making field trips together for a couple of years when he reached into a drawer in his office in Laramie and handed me a journal that had been started by his mother long before she was married—when she had first come to Wyoming. She had been born more than 100 years before I saw her manuscript, and needless to say I never met her, but, as I have noted elsewhere, the admiration and affection I came to feel toward her is probably matched by no one I've encountered in my professional life. This was not merely because she had the courage to venture as a young teacher into very distant country, or because she later educated her own bright children, or because she was more than equal to the considerable difficulties of ranch subsistence, but also because she recorded these things—in her journals and later writings—with such wit, insight, grace, irony, compassion, sarcasm, stylistic elegance and embracing humor that I could not resist her.

Her unpublished journal was a large gift to me, and with the permission of her son and daughter I used fragments from it to help recreate her family's world. My work, though, did not include a hundredth part of what was there. My presentation could only suggest her. In years that have followed, two of her granddaughters have sifted through attics and other archives to discover packets of letters to and from her, various forms of writing by and about her and another journal. Their work in arranging, annotating, and editing what they found has not only been loving in nature but restrainedly skillful in accomplishment. In "Lady's Choice," they have elected to present her between 1905, when she began her first journal, and 1910, when she decided to marry John Galloway Love, a cowboy from Scotland who, in the Wind River Basin of Wyoming, had presented his credentials to her seemingly within moments of her arrival. The boundaries of this volume (another will follow) are deliberate and significant, for they enclose a young American woman of nearly a century ago in something like a complex of competing magnets. Self-possessed, cool, detached, she clearly knows that this is her time, and she takes it. As this chronological flow of journal entries, letters and poems progresses, she is not only wooed by the cowboy but also importuned by a Wyoming mother who sees the young schoolteacher as a match for her own son, and who attempts to assassinate the character of John Love by referring to him as a gossip. Possibly she helps to effectuate a marriage she hopes to prevent. Letters are arriving all the while from Wellesley friends who are now in places like medical school and Paris. She experiments with teaching jobs in other states, in one instance at a sort of nunnery in Wisconsin, with macabre, humorous results. Always, she is writing—an incidental skill that would later become an ambition. Always, as well, John Love is writing to her. Indirectly, she is being asked to choose between a very isolated family life and the realm of other possibilities easily within reach of (as someone puts it in a letter to John Love) "her combination of strength and the gentlest charm—welded by that flashing mind."

Recently, when her granddaughters sent to me the annotated manuscript of this volume, I raced through the innumerable letters and the later journal that I had never seen, looking for that flashing mind and the person I felt I knew. When she described one of the faculty members at the school in Wisconsin as "a square prunes-and-prisms lady with a mouth like a buttonhole," I was reassured that I had found her.

Elsewhere, when a difficult woodstove at last began to function properly, she wrote, "The stove has developed a conscience."

When she taught Latin and Greek for a time at Central High School in Pueblo, Colorado, and lived in the home of one Mrs. Butler, she wrote to John Love:

> Mrs. Butler ... is a little war-horse of a woman with a long, thin husband. I'm telling you about her, because she has been improving him for about 20 years, and it is beginning to tell on him.

Reading again the journal that she kept when she was 23, I found everywhere the sense of landscape that resembled her touch with people:

> The dampness had brought out the darkness of the red soil, and the blackness of the green cedars. The sagebrush, too, along the way, was as black about the branches as if a fire had passed over the hills. The bluffs loomed dark and moody against the gray sky, but far away at the Big Bend the hills were the color of pale straw. The mountain looked yellowish green, softened by a sifting of snow. It is strange how the whole face of the country will be changed by a little dampness, like the face of a person intensified but softened by tears.

It should be said that while this lady's choice was a classic dilemma, John Love's side of it was something close to an all-or-nothing gamble. He was 35 years old when he fell in love with her. He lived in a place so far from community that he did not glimpse a woman for months at a time. He presented himself to her without guile, and she dealt in kind with him. For five years, he took no for an answer but never changed his question. When his letters developed closing salutations that were unacceptably intimate—for example, "Ever Yours"—and she verbally rapped his knuckles for it, thereafter he said, "Sincerely." Abidingly, he carried within him the heart and the humor, not to mention the brain, of the Scots. He was a match for her. Evidently, she knew it.

As this volume ends, she accepts him, his ranch and a fulfillable vision of their life together. Her granddaughters quote from something she wrote years later, describing an embroidered sampler that existed only in her imagination and depicted the ranch and its hands and her family and certain symbols of a time in the Wind River Basin.

I will wait impatiently for the sampler. Meanwhile, these distinct themes from her single life will more than do.

Incidental remarks at Columbia University, November 19, 1987, the day Robert Giroux receives the university's Alexander Hamilton Award, highest honor given to an alumnus:

As everyone knows at Farrar, Straus & Giroux, Roger Straus was born in a Guggenheim mine with a copper spoon in his mouth. It's still lying around somewhere, and the only way to get his ear is to find the spoon and put it back.

What people don't know is that a piece of wild country called Giroux Wash, Nev., was the scene of a gold strike at the end of the 19th century by the brothers E.L. Giroux and Joseph Giroux, whose 109 claims bore literary names like Vendetta, Victor Hugo and Jane Grey, not to mention the name of their discovery claim, which they simply called Giroux. The underlying rock was the Arcturus Formation. The Giroux brothers sank something called the Giroux Shaft—1,440 feet. They set up the Giroux Concentrator—500 pounds a day. Their Giroux Consolidated Mines not only brought forth deep royalties of gold but, in time, a billion dollars' worth of copper.

Had these unclaimed ancestors appeared in Union Square, we would now be working for Giroux, Giroux & Giroux. As it happens, though, Bob has never heard of them—not before this moment. They were recently and inadvertently discovered for him by a Princeton University geologist who, with the backing of a Columbia University alumnus-entrepreneur, has been staking new gold claims in the general vicinity of Giroux Wash, where mineable assays exist in a form of deposit that could not have been detected by 19th-century prospectors. A claims-staking war is in progress right now, and the Princeton-Columbia forces seem to be winning. With Columbia supplying the seed money and Princeton the other essential component, fresh millions may soon be added to the Columbia endowment.

Aware of tonight's event and the Alexander Hamilton Award, the Princeton geologist, Ken Deffeyes, hiked into Giroux Wash a couple of weeks ago and picked up a rock. He brought it home, sliced it, lacquered it, labeled it, and has given it to me to give, with his congratulations, to Bob Giroux. It may or may not contain gold, but a rock, whatever it contains, seems an appropriate gift for an author to present to a publisher. Particularly, this rock. It is chalcedony, mother of flint, chert and jasper. Its lyrical, metaphorical family name is cryptocrystalline quartz.

As I deliver it with guileless affection, I wish to assure all Columbia College alumni, and especially Robert Giroux, that there is absolutely no truth to the rumor that Princeton, in honor of one of its sons, has established the Aaron Burr Award for Marksmanship.

Tom Eglin's sense of humor, sharp enough in the first place, remarkably seemed to rise—to become increasingly rich in perception and range—in response to his besetting illness. I hope I won't be misunderstood when I say that Tom was an easy patient to visit. He was wry. He was funny. He was anecdotal. He cheered *you* up. He told *you* stories. There was a basketball backboard in his bedroom with a berserk little ball. He counted up, with amusement, the shots *you* missed.

Mindful of our common Scottish backgrounds—his even closer in time than mine—he told me a story about taking his sons on a voyage among the isles of Scotland. An educational cruise it was, professors aboard, a ship called Argonaut, a captain who was not called Jason. As the boys sailed into the very waters of their heritage, they were seasick. This, as they had read, was "the land of the bens and the glens, where not even Sir Walter Scott could exaggerate the romantic beauty of that lake and mountain country penetrated by fjords that came in from seas that were starred with islands. The weather changes so abruptly there—closing in, lifting, closing in again—that all in an hour wind-driven rain may be followed by calm and hazy sunshine, which may then be lost in heavy mists that soon disappear into open skies over dark-blue seas. When the ocean is blue, the air is as pure as a lens, and the islands seem imminent and almost encroaching, although they are 10 or 15 miles away—Mull, for example, Scarba, Islay, Jura, the Isles of the Sea." With all that off the starboard rail, the boys were seasick; and when they were finished being seasick, they came down with flu and went into steerage in the hold. Telling the story with a slight blush and smile, Tom confessed annoyance. He said that he had been, in fact, profoundly irritated by his sons' becoming sick, "because the trip, as you can imagine, was not inexpensive." This was one Scottish father speaking to another directly from the heart.

When Bill Bradley came to Princeton, Tom was his freshman adviser, Tom's mission being to guide this aimless youth toward some sort of utilitarian destiny. Evidently, Tom succeeded. It was the beginning of an enduring friendship, and Tom's encouragement and generosity of counsel were prized by Bill from then to now. From time to time, our three paths crossed. When Bill was in college, and practicing by himself one summer in the Lawrenceville field house, he missed six jump shots in a row. He said to us, "You want to know something? That basket is about an inch and a half low." Some days later, Tom got a stepladder, and he and I measured the basket. It was one and one-eighth inches too low. When Bill was an NBA basketball player, in the early 1970s, he occasionally went to Lawrenceville to practice alone. One day, feeding the ball back to him, I developed a grandiose fantasy. "Suppose I were somehow to get into a game with you in Madison Square Garden," I said. "Could you get *me* a shot in the NBA?" "Of course," he said, and he sketched out a certain baseline move by which a person 2 feet tall could score on Abdul-Jabbar. At that moment, out of nowhere, Tom appeared. Bradley told him to guard me, and the play worked. Tom and I reversed roles, and the play worked—the play being so ambiguous that I couldn't stop it even though I knew what was going to happen. Now two people whose height added up to a single basketball player's would forever be grateful to Bill for their one and only shot in the NBA.

Those are just a couple of reminiscences from one person who first knew Tom in college and later was his frequent tennis partner for 10 or 15 years, including a time when I most especially needed a friend, and in his quiet way, without a great deal actually said, he was right there. Comparable streams of remembrance surround each one of us at this time, all as different and particular as they would be analogous, all relating to this bright figure of quiet humor—this athlete, counselor, teacher—whose capacity for love and friendship were outsized.

I used to go to New Hampshire in the summertime with a stack of New Yorkers a foot and a half high. I would paddle straight over the lake until I was 27 yards out of earshot, and then I would lie down and go through those magazines like a drill bit, looking for things I particularly remembered, looking for things I'd missed on journeys during the year. Trillin in Provence fighting bulls in water—*Taureaux Piscine!* Mark Singer and the Puerto Rican rooster in the window of the Israeli locksmith shop on Seventh Avenue. Ackerman and the albatross, Iglauer and the salmon, Frazier's metaphysical bears. Barich up, in the eighth at Santa Anita, wearing our silks. Updike on the eighth, parring. Angell in the eighth, relieving.

Finished with the animals, I started on the vegetables, and once in a while I paddled ashore and called up The New Yorker library. Hello, Helen, in what issue did Whiteside tee up the American-latex tomato? Whose was the thing about the grass at Wimbledon? When was Kahn in the rice paddy? Helen Stark knew everything, but her line was often busy with calls from other canoes.

Speaking of libraries: A big open-stack academic or public library is no small pleasure to work in. You're, say, trying to do a piece on something in Nevada, and you go down to C Floor, deep in the earth, and out to what a miner would call a remote working face. You find 10995.497S just where the card catalog and the on-line computer thought it would be, but that is only the initial nick. The book you knew about has led you to others you did not know about. To the ceiling the shelves are loaded with books about Nevada. You pull them down, one at a time, and sit on the floor and look them over until you are sitting on a pile 5 feet high, at which point you are late home for dinner and you get up and walk away. It's an incomparable boon to research, all that; but it is also a reason why there are almost no large open-stack libraries left in the world.

I have worked for 20 years in the East Pyne building at Princeton, in a corridor dominated by the Department of Comparative Literature, where the Humanities Council (my employer) has a small inholding. Comp Lit has had two chairmen in its history at Princeton: Robert Fagles, whose translation of Homer is a work still in progress, and Robert Hollander, curator of Dante. As both are overly fond of saying, I am an interloper there, a fake professor, a portfolio without minister. For all that, the third floor of East Pyne is a superb place to work. By 6:30 p.m., it is essentially vacant. Only Roger Mudd and I are there—the unofficials, the visiting professors. Even the tenure track is quietly rusting. At 7:30 a.m., though, a lonely figure will be wandering the hall—the back arched, the head a little cocked, the lips in perpetual motion—mumbling about warriors armed in bronze. He understands bronze. Anyone with that much brass would understand bronze. Long ago I learned that if you hear Fagles coming, step into the corridor, and confront him with a question, he turns into an ambulatory checking department, a mine of antique material, the willing donor in an act of cerebral osmosis. For example, there came a time when my geological compositions became focused on a passage about the island of Cyprus. I heard him coming, stepped into the hall, and later went back to my machine and wrote: "In 2760 B.C., smelting began in Cyprus. Slag heaps developed in 40 places. "The Iliad" is populated with warriors armed in bronze. Bronze is copper hardened by adding some tin, and the copper would have come from Cyprus. (Copper was mined on Cyprus for nearly 2,000 years before Homer.) ... The word 'Cyprus' means copper. Whether the island is named for the metal or the metal for the island is an etymology lost in time."

When I bring Fagles fish from the Delaware River, as I sometimes do, he asks that they be gutted, finned, beheaded, and scaled, and wrapped in my work.

He was reputedly squeamish, a little shy, about gore in any form. He liked his cornflakes well done. When I was in the process of writing a piece about a woman who collected roadkills and skinned them out for a university but ate their bodies for her own nourishment and pleasure, his hovering image, to say the least, was never out of mind. He would be reader No. 1. I had not known of my subject's diet when I proposed the story to him. Now he would decide whether the piece would appear in his magazine. The pan-fried snakes and the weasels en brochette had to get past him.

I sent him the manuscript expecting it to remain in that state forever. After a while, he called. "Well," he said, "I liked your story...." He broke off for a long pause. Then he said: "No. I didn't like your story. I could hardly read it. But that woman is closer to the earth than I am. Her work is significant. I'm pleased to publish the piece."

A year or two later, writing about Alaska, I mentioned the truly dreadful packaged food that I had eaten on a government expedition in the Brooks Range, including things like freeze-dried eggs and cold, pink-icinged pop tarts with raspberry filling. I also mentioned that the forest eskimos of the Kobuk Valley were especially fond of the fat that lies behind a caribou's eye. I posed this question: "To a palate without bias—the palate of an open-minded Berber, the palate of a travelling Martian—which would be the more acceptable, a pink-icinged pop tart with raspberry filling (cold) or the fat gob behind a caribou's eye?"

The editor of the piece was Robert Bingham, but there was, always, something known as "the Shawn proof." In the margin beside that great philosophical question, he had written, in his small hand: "The pop tart."

He was in the great line of leaders who see no succession. As he advanced in years, though, the question of what would happen next grew around him like a rind. Now and again, with craft, he reacted. In the 1970s, at least 10 years before he actually retired and 50 before he meant to retire, he called me (and many other writers) and said that he thought the time had come to spread some of his usual functions, strategically hinting that retirement was what he had in mind. He said that from then on I would not be conversing directly with him about editorial matters but should address myself instead to Mr. Bingham or Mr. Crow. Only at certain times, he said, would he be dealing directly with me, and those occasions would be, first, when I had an idea for a story and wished to propose it; second, when I had a completed manuscript to give to him; and third, when the story went to press.

He understood the disjunct kinship of creative work—every kind of creative work—and time. The most concise summation of it I've ever heard were seven words he said just before closing my first profile and sending it off to press. I was a new young writer, 1965, and he did not entrust new writers to any extent whatever to other editors. He got the new ones started by himself. So there we were—hours at a session—discussing reverse pivots and back-door plays and the role of the left-handed comma in the architectonics of basketball while The New Yorker hurtled toward its deadlines. I finally had to ask him, "How can you afford to use so much time and go into so many things in such detail when this whole enterprise is yours to keep together?"

He said, "It takes as long as it takes."

As a part-time writing teacher, I have offered those words to a generation of students. If they are writers, they will never forget it.

I hope you don't mind if I speak from notes. In an author-publisher relationship of nearly 30 years, this is the first opportunity I have had to get some words in edgewise, and I don't want to let even one of them get away.

Last fall, after I was invited by Bob Moskin to join Tom Wolfe in speaking here at a Lotos Club dinner honoring Roger Straus, Roger Straus soon called me to say that this was entirely the club's idea, "etcetera, etcetera, and so forth, and so on," and definitely not his idea. "In fact," he said, "I told them I didn't think you were very bright." He said that he did not want me to feel any obligation whatsoever to him. There was no need for me to have to come all the way in from Princeton. Etcetera, etcetera. And so forth, and so on.

I said, "That's not the issue, Roger. That's not what we're discussing. What I need to know is, Is it all right to say 'Fuck you' in the Lotos Club?"

He said, "I see the lines along which you are thinking. Of course it's all right. It's perfectly all right. And, besides, you're not a member."

When I was quite young, I was inadvertently armored for a future with Roger Straus. My grandfather was a publisher. My uncle was a publisher. The house was the John C. Winston Book and Bible Company, of Philadelphia, Pennsylvania, and they published the "Silver Chief" series, about a sled dog in the frozen north. That dog was my boyhood hero. One day, I was saddened to see in a newspaper that Jack O'Brien, the author of those books, had died. A couple of years passed. I went into high school. The publishing company became Holt, Rinehart & Winston, and my Uncle Bob's office moved to New York. When I was visiting him there one day, a man arrived for an appointment, and Uncle Bob said, "John, meet Jack O'Brien, the author of 'Silver Chief.'" I shook the author's hand, which wasn't very cold. After he had gone, I said, "Uncle Bob, I thought Jack O'Brien died."

Uncle Bob said, "He did die. He died. Actually, we've had three or four Jack O'Briens. Let me tell you something, John. Authors are a dime a dozen. The dog is immortal."

I have now dealt with Roger Straus in all or parts of four decades without an agent. I have never had another publisher. When I signed up with Roger Straus, in 1965, I was 6 feet 7 inches tall. The less than modest height of the man you see before you is a direct result of that relationship. We have done upwards of 20 books together, and contractual negotiations take place in private conversation between us. Like the lawyer who takes himself for a client, I have risked foolishness. I once asked Roger, "How much money am I losing as a result of not having an agent?" And he answered, "Oh, not a whole hell of a lot."

One of the people I have most admired was a writer who knew how to fly and rented an airplane in which he attacked Simon and Schuster. I have long advised Roger to keep an eye on his window.

One time, when he was contracting to publish a hefty hardcover book with my name on it as author, I asked him for an advance, and he said, "Fuck you." So help me, that is what he said.

Truth be told, though, the book was a "reader," an amalgam of fragments of other books, for which he had long since paid advances. On an earlier occasion—in 1967—when we talked about publishing what was to be my fifth book but first collection of short miscellaneous pieces, I said to him, "This one isn't going to make a nickel. Collections never do. I'm grateful to you just for publishing it. Don't bother to pay me an advance."

"Nonsense," he said. "I'm your publisher. Of course, I will pay you an advance. I insist." And he named a sum which, in present company, I am somewhat shy to reveal. Let us just say that it was in two figures.

In fact, it was $1,500. The book was published in 1968. It did not do well over the counter. It took 14 years to earn back the $1,500. Notice something, though: After all those years, it was in print. Commercially, that book could not have been a bigger dog if its title were "Remainder." In conglomerate publishing, it would have vanished three weeks after it was published. But somebody kept it in print, as he has kept all my books —marginal and otherwise, hardcover and soft—in print. When I cash Roger's checks, I can hear the tellers giggling as I walk away, but even in my Scottish core I really don't care. In 1991, in its 23rd year, that ancient collection of miscellaneous pieces sold 700 copies. A small figure. But for that book—for any trade book—23 years is an amazing longevity. Thanks entirely to its publisher. The dog is immortal.

Seventeen years ago, I began teaching a course in factual writing as a visiting professor at Princeton. To every group of students I have taught, Roger Straus has come and talked nonstop—"etcetera, etcetera, and so forth, and so on"—for three hours at a crack, with a cumulative rate of repetition of 4 percent. He repeatedly came to the course in a period when his health was inconvenienced by a good deal more than a cold. The students are prepared to interview him, but one question is always enough. "Could you tell us about Alexander Solzhenitsyn?" someone asks. And Roger says, "Eighteen years ago, when I first started having serious intercourse with the big A....," and he's off and running for three hours of free association.

I've given up on the attack plane. I have decided in the end to strafe him here with words, to embarrass him with words of an appropriate sort that he least knows how to handle, words that describe the invaluable in his gift and his giving as a publisher: care, for example, encouragement, counsel, anticipation, thoughtfulness, amenity and reassurance, loquacity and spirit, accommodation, reinforcement, vision, foresight, hindsight, sensibility, solicitude, affection, application, waggery, levity, boldness, courage, intrepidity, optimism, consolation, earthiness, ribaldry, decency, vulgarity, sorcery, alchemy, hoodoo, voodoo, conviviality, comicality, whimsicality, farcicality, fraternity and friendship, not to mention what I calculate to have been (over the years, and largely on the telephone) 1,000 hours of a dialogue too good to be printable.

Tom and I are here because Tom is the house eagle and I am the company mule. I say that with no false humility. I say it as plain fact. I would not know how to light a bonfire if someone handed me the match. I write about geology. In a sense, I am selling rocks. In Union Square, I know a sucker who will buy them.

John McPhee *is the author of more than 20 books of nonfiction; his latest volume is entitled "Irons in the Fire." He teaches writing at Princeton University.*

Cover to Cover
Reviews of New Books

The Miss Dennis School of Writing and Other Lessons From a Woman's Life

By Alice Steinbach   *The Bancroft Press, 307 pp*

In her first book, a collection of funny and poignant essays, Alice Steinbach uses a voice that is conversational and confidential. A Pulitzer Prize-winning writer for The Baltimore Sun, Steinbach surveys the sexes, fashion, adolescence, lessons from motherhood, heroines, special places and losses.

The essay that inspires the book's title is excellent. Miss Dennis, who was Steinbach's creative writing teacher in high school, pushed her to discover her own voice, something many aspiring writers never learn. In a conversation with this memorable mentor, Steinbach confides her grief about her father's death during this well-drawn scene:

"I shall never forget that late fall afternoon; the sound of the vanilla-colored blinds flap, flap, flapping in the still classroom; the sun falling in shafts through the windows, each ray illuminating tiny galaxies of chalk dust in the air; the smell of wet blackboards; the

teacher, small with apricot-colored hair, listening intently to a young girl blurting out her grief."

In the Miss Dennis essay and others in this collection, Steinbach is as reflective as Anna Quindlen. She also can be as quick-witted as Dorothy Parker. Loneliness, a common theme in Parker's short stories, figures prominently in an essay called "At the Beauty Spa."

Steinbach spends Thanksgiving Day at the Greenhouse, an exclusive spa for women in Dallas, Texas. The piece conjures up mental images of the "social X-rays" Tom Wolfe satirized in "The Bonfire of the Vanities." These are women who are so focused on being thin and beautiful that they neglect their inner selves. Steinbach's dinner companion, who wears a tiara, confides that she spends every Thanksgiving at the spa.

One of the very best pieces is "The Girl Who Loved Cats and Flowers." In the fall of 1984, Steinbach's mother began writing an account of her life. Three months later, in December, she died of cancer. Drawing on her mother's story and notes from her own journal, Steinbach weaves a sensitive account of her mother's courage and how she dealt with her grief after her mother's death.

Like her hero, E.B. White, Steinbach is capable of finding large truths in small events such as planting flowers with her son or advising a bunch of teen-aged girls how to wear their hair for the prom. In "Lost and Found," she describes the sudden, mysterious disappearance of many small appliances from her home. Then, she relates her wry amusement at eating popcorn out of her popper while visiting her son at college.

The weakest essay is the story of Kimberly Erica May's death from cancer. While Steinbach catalogs May's accomplishments and says she had "an arresting face," we never get a clear image of her as we do with Miss Dennis.

Steinbach is a fine essayist because she is willing to reveal her weaknesses as well as her strengths in life. Her self-deprecating humor shows that she is able to laugh at herself. I look forward to reading her next book, "Journal of a Dangerous Woman."

—*Marylynne Pitz*

That Shining Place
By Simone Poirier-Bures

Oberon Press, 93 pp

Winner of the 1995 Evelyn Richardson Memorial Literary Award (Canada's most prestigious award for nonfiction), Simone Poirier-Bures' memoir, "That Shining Place," recalls a three-month period the author lived on the island of Crete during the winter of 1965-66 and details the author's return trip to the island in 1991. This brief book of only 93 pages engages a surprising range of concerns, including the materialism of North American culture; the difficulties in negotiating the cultural differences between 1960s Greece and Canada; a cross-cultural friendship between the author and a local Greek woman; and the reconciliation of the author's memory of the 1960s island with 1990s reality.

The author's time in Greece ("the scene of my life's great adventure, my life's great experiment") is a pivotal moment in her life, and the strength of the memoir comes from the effective use of counterpoint between the wise post-Greece point of view and the innocent self's experience of the island for the first time. The author alternates sections between these two points of view. The author's trip to Greece was a search. "It is 1966 and I am 21. I am in Chania, on the island of Crete, searching for something. Some truth that keeps eluding me. Some peace I long for. I am fleeing old griefs, trying to lose myself, find myself." On her return in 1991 the author is still searching but this time for reconciliation of her two selves, pre- and post-Greece. "It seems hardly possible that my younger self and I could have inhabited the same body, the same life. ... I wanted both Apollo and Dionysius—order and unboundedness. How did the two exist? And how could I reconcile them within myself? The answer had to be here somewhere." The hope for reconciliation motivates not only the return trip to Greece but also the composition of the memoir.

The most significant relationship revealed in the memoir is between the author and a Greek housewife. "Maria was my guide, lifting up the corners of her world, letting me in." Maria remains important for the author upon her return. "I have come back to Crete searching for something I have lost. She will know where it is." This

relationship, like the author's feelings for the shining place, was destined for disillusionment. "I was not for her what she was for me; I have not inhabited her life the way she has inhabited mine." This disillusionment proves essential in the author's reconciliation of the two halves of her self.

The shining place of the book's title not only describes the village of Chania, but also Maria's kitchen, the shining place that the memory of this time in Greece has held for the author, and ultimately the shining place the book creates for the reader. Unfortunately, the inclusion of an afterword titled "Writing 'The Greece Piece'" draws attention away from the shining places suggested by the book's title. In lifting this veil on her creative process, the author does a disservice to her powerful foregoing narrative.

—*Carlos L. Dews*

Immortelles: *Memoir of a Will-o'-the-Wisp*
By Mireille Marokvia   *MacMurray & Beck, Inc., 130 pp*

"Immortelles" is a small, seductive book. The childhood recollections of Mireille Marokvia are written in clear and often lyrical prose. She offers glimpses of her young life in a tiny French village near Chartres in the early years of this century in roughly chronological order, but (as her subtitle suggests) in calling herself a will-o'-the-wisp she has given herself permission to be the feu follet

or foolish fire, the little light appearing, disappearing and reappearing, dancing among gravestones and across marshes, warning us that memory is selective, recollection idiosyncratic.

This is not to say that the reader questions the veracity of her memories. Quite the opposite. When she isn't sure or can't quite remember she says so. Freud claims that we are all haunted houses, and

Marokvia ends her prologue by stating, "I still have some remembering to do. My ghosts are demanding their shred of immortality." And that she gives them. Immortelles or everlastings, the little straw flowers traditionally strewn on graves in rural France, provide not just the title but the book's controlling metaphor. They allow Marokvia to ask the question, more of herself and of her readers than of French country people, "Why, why do freethinkers who do not believe in immortality feel that they have to bury their dead under a blanket of immortelles?" Her memoir addresses the very real human need to believe our lives have meaning and suggests that the act of writing itself confers a "shred of immortality" on both writer and subject. The writer of memoir may also find a version of the philosopher's stone—"Losses turned to riches through the singular alchemy that we choose to call memory."

Yet as memoir, lived in French but written in English many decades later, "Immortelles" raises some interesting questions: What does it mean to write in a language very different from the one in which the thinking, speaking, listening, writing, learning, loving and hating were actually experienced? By recalling a life in other than the language which informed it, can the writer add a protective layer between the written memoir and the felt memory? The answer is probably not. We know it wasn't possible for Conrad, even in his fiction. His work is clearly fueled by his life experiences before he ever learned English. And contemporary novelist Amy Tan's work succeeds in its emotional impact in large part because it is steeped in the language and traditions of her ancestors. Yet Marokvia's long life makes the time/space/place link with language and identity an especially intriguing one.

The epilogue, written from Marokvia's home in New Mexico in March 1996, offers hints about her next volume of reflections—her marriage to a German artist and their years in Germany during World War II. We look forward to meeting other old ghosts through her magical method of conferring immortality.

—*Margaret D. Sullivan*

Place of the Pretend People: *Gifts from a Yup'ik Eskimo Village*
By Carolyn Kremers   *Alaska Northwest Books, 238 pp*

In this foggy, cold, extremely windy village (windchill often brings the temperature down to 90 degrees below zero) of Tununak, "...hugging the edges of Nelson Island and the Bering Sea like a child hugging her elders," Carolyn Kremers opens herself to living with the Yup'ik Indians, teaching English and music, and absorbing their way of life.

Kremers' two years with the people and with the land itself, and perhaps her musical training, infuse her memoir with a finely-tuned receptiveness for the voices around her. Tununak villagers would talk about seal hunting, ice fishing, dancing, music and getting back their culture and language. We hear the elders speak eloquently of the incompatibility that exists between Alaskan Native traditions of consensus decision-making and of sharing property and traditional attitudes toward stewardship of the land and sea and the federal government's attempts to incorporate ownership of the land into a hierarchial structure which the people fear will do irreparable harm. Her pointed and poetic comments about all she sees and hears complete the circle which these native voices from the village have begun.

Kremers writes with emotion and insight when she describes the traditional rituals of ceremonial dancing and drumming she witnesses in the village: "Though I could not see it, Yup'ik dancing glowed like a banked fire inside the children and teenagers I taught every day at school. This music was part of Tununak people's collective unconscious, I thought, like Bach was part of mine."

Yet it seems Kremers is writing another memoir within this memoir of the villagers and her experience in Tununak. It is almost as if she finds her truest pitch when she travels away from the village and into the wilderness. Have the months teaching and learning the

traditions of the Yup'ik allowed her to become open to this deeper voice inside her? Perhaps the quiet, cold, winter days and nights on the Bering coast permitted her passage to the unknown wilderness inside her which she must and does finally discover.

Whatever the reasons, her writing reaches its highest level of excitement and brilliance when she is traveling through the Alaskan wilderness with her lover. It is in these chapters that her writing achieves a singular harmony of place that connects her and the reader to every beautifully rendered detail, and has readers wishing there was even more.

Throughout the book, when Kremers is living in the village, teaching, visiting the people in their homes, attending dancing ceremonies, shopping in the town store, she is very conscious of her aloneness and of her independence. When she is camping with her lover, Dan, she is quite dependent on him, yet her writing becomes most alive, most poignant, most evocative. She seems to enter fully into her environment, not only sharply imparting each detail to the reader, but also emotionally integrating her own experience, so we no longer feel her sense of "otherness" and the cultural distance from that which she is describing.

Kremers writes of this time in the Alaskan wilderness as if she were experiencing a soulful symphonic movement, her ear so well-trained that each instrument is distinct and separate, yet all, including herself, are in concert. On her two trips with Dan, a cross-country race which ends in their having to be rescued by seaplane, and a "pulking" trip, a method of pulling gear on sleds behind skis, Kremers fascinates her readers with her wonderful awareness of all that surrounds her: for the ordinary never-ending work of a camping trip, for the scent of the pine boughs they cut to use as a mattress under their tent, for her squeamishness as Dan fells a live tree for firewood, and simply for how she feels at any given moment. When she almost falls into the ice as she tries to fill a water bottle, Dan rebukes her for her carelessness, and she writes: "He's right to have gotten upset with me.

I frightened him. Clarity comes to a fast-beating heart."

Dan is larger than life, a Viking-like figure, and with him Kremers seems to reach a highly sensitized state of awareness. Her narrative becomes magical in these moments: "In the evening it starts snowing on the campfire. Snow falls all night, and all the next day and the next night. You can hear crystals sprinkling on the tent under the tree."

"Place of the Pretend People" is a penetrating memoir of a woman's discovery process into the music of the self and the voices of another people. Her greatest discovery is that she understands that the Yup'ik people of Tununak and the Bering coast tundra have found their way inside her and will always be there, "... even when I think I am alone."

—*Kenneth Boas*

Born Southern and Restless
By Kat Meads

Duquesne University Press, 224 pp

Kat Meads' first collection of essays begins with an explanation of "The Itch of Wanderlust" she shares with her brother: "... when my favorite bookstore goes out of business, or the quality of lettuce and pears deteriorates at Craig's favorite market, or we've simply seen all we wanted to see ... we'll give in to the itch of wanderlust." In little more than 200 pages, Meads applies such a no-nonsense credo to nearly 30 essays filled with the people and places that have inhabited her

dynamic notion of home. "Born Southern and Restless" neither lingers in any particular place too long, nor treads the border of sentimentality.

Although the book begins by admitting to the allure of the unfamiliar, most of the essays in the first half stay close to Meads' rural upbringing in Shawboro, N.C. With clarity and judicious detail, Kat Meads renders spare portraits of family, community and her own fond memories of the quick, small moments of childhood. Readers are shown a younger Meads who tries to join her church at the age of 6 and is finally baptized in a nearby lake at 13. We see her place third in a tainted spelling bee, shoot hoops with her family in a friendly game of "Horse," spend summer evenings in a Nag's Head bar, and we feel both her fear of and attraction to the snake-haunted waters near her home.

While the Southern landscape and its surrounding customs emerge as minor characters, Meads' recollections most often hinge on family members. She writes of a fishing trip through the character of her father, "... someone who can fish for hours without taking a Pepsi break, who can locate round robin in an east wind, who can land bait between water lilies blooming 6 inches apart." One of the most idiosyncratic and resonant of the relatives is her grandmother, Dora. When a stranger approaches Dora "with a basket of fruit and New Testament tracts," she responds unequivocally. With a butcher knife in hand, she shoos the misguided "do-gooder of the Lord" away: "'Come round again ... and we'll see about those skinny fingers of yours.'" In such moments, Meads' writing shows the integrity of its promise: What you see is what you get. The matter-of-fact language Meads uses helps to convey how important, familiar and underrated the ordinary elements of childhood are.

When Meads' focus drifts away from Shawboro in the second half of the collection and skips from one part of the country to another, the reader understands the particular background that has trained her vision. Most of the subsequent essays offer thin, clipped descriptions of what she meets in her "wanderlust." Encounters are often framed around Meads' own varied employment, from potato handler to dog groomer. The quick pace is sustained through the end of the collection with spontaneous shifts in focus and stream-of-conscious structures.

There are times when Meads' reticence to linger, to probe beneath the surface, or to infuse the benefit of retrospect weakens her writing. These essays occasionally conclude by raising questions that might mean more if they were answered, and as a result, some opportunities are eclipsed. Such is the case in "The Coupling and the Un," which concludes with speculation: "Maybe their relationship remained rock solid. Maybe it was the work of glue. Maybe, all along, it was pure facade." In "Joe, Leo and Lillian," Meads details a local murder trial that took place when she was in high school. She seems content without any answers: "I have no valid access." One sometimes wishes that she would push harder, risk more by writing beyond the question and towards an answer.

In the end, Meads' ambition to cover so much ground becomes an obstacle. In rendering so many people and places, the reader is often left looking for connections that do not surface. Still, these essays work hard to illuminate the extraordinary in the familiar, to uncover the familiar in the foreign, and finally depend upon Meads' just telling. Frequently, they succeed.

—*Kathleen Veslany*

Castles Burning: A Child's Life in War
By Magda Denes

W. W. Norton & Company, 384 pp

Magda Denes is the precocious child/narrator of this deeply rewarding memoir about her Jewish family's suffering under fascism in Hungary in the early 1940s. Magda, whom her mother once described as "big-mouthed, insolent and far too smart," is a privileged, imaginative and witty child whose secure and magical world is replaced by a nightmare of persecution, displacement, and loss. An angry Magda protests that "God was not in his Heaven," during those wartime years when she and her family go into hiding from the fascist Arrow-Cross. If, as Graham Greene wrote, "Exile is deprivation," Magda's family is in exile long before their odyssey ends, or perhaps begins anew, in Cuba, where they arrive as refugees in 1947.

When her beloved older brother and mentor, Ivan, is murdered during one of the capricious and deadly assaults on Jewish citizens, Magda realizes that the merits of moral, intellectual and physical fitness do not qualify one for survival. Though convinced that "contingency, chance, and the accidental circumstance determine fate," she and her family, fearful and exhausted by perpetual physical, spiritual

and emotional hardship, choose tenacity and resourcefulness over self-pity. They become adept at reinventing their identities and changing location frequently, hiding in the attics of Christian friends, or in a safe house where, as home to 3,500 frightened, filthy, hungry people, the "smell is corporeal in its rankness." Responding to the dissolution of all familiar routine, Magda learns to speak and behave according to the exigencies of each new crisis, to lie, to feign confidence, to modulate her movements and edit her interactions; she becomes an expert in deception by denying truth, her heritage, selfhood, pain, and childhood needs. "I knew the world and I had ceased to be contiguous. ... Everything I had ever known had lost its fixity."

The events in Magda Denes' story are tragically familiar as the consequences of persecution and conflict. What distinguishes her account from many others is her determination to tell the truth not as historical fact but as history as it is *experienced*; this is not a mimetic retelling nor the reminiscential impressionism of many memoirs. Denes' recollections are synthesized into a seamless and psychologically convincing narrative, the dialogical passages reflecting the complex interactions, moral uncertainties and emotional ambiguities of real relationships. Family members are described with a loving candor which doesn't spare their foibles or resist their charms; Denes' fierce commitment to veracity would never permit sentimental revision of her past, although her compassion is evident on every page.

"Castles Burning" is a testimony to the preservation of history through language and an assertion that the speaker, the witness, must be responsible to both history and language in order to get it right. The beauty of Denes' writing is not the beauty of poetry but rather the eloquence of a deeply intelligent and moral response to personal and historic tragedy and loss; Magda Denes is a remembrancer who has refused to allow the past to claim her lost childhood and loved ones a second time.

Magda Denes is a psychoanalyst in private practice in New York City.
—Lea Simonds

Marylynne Pitz *is a staff writer at the Pittsburgh Post-Gazette.*

Carlos L. Dews *is an assistant professor of American Literature in the Department of English and Foreign Languages at the University of West Florida.*

Margaret D. Sullivan *is a freelance writer who teaches at Hunter College.*

Kenneth Boas *teaches in the English Department at La Roche College.*

Kathleen Veslany *received her MFA from the University of Pittsburgh where she now teaches.*

Lea Simonds *is a member of the Editorial Advisory Board of Creative Nonfiction.*

The Colgate University

Chenango Valley Writers' Conference

June 29 – July 5, 1997

Staff:
Peter Balakian
David Bradley
Frederick Busch
Deborah Digges
Reginald McKnight
Leila Philip
Hilma Wolitzer

Publishing:
Jill Bialosky, Norton
Stanley W. Lindberg,
 Georgia Review
Elaine Markson, Elaine
 Markson Literary Agency
Alice Quinn, *The New Yorker*
Michael Seidman, Walker
 & Co.

Workshops, individual
conferences, craft talks,
panels. Air-conditioned
classrooms, library and
computer lab. Hiking,
boating, fitness center,
swimming.

Contact:
Frederick Busch,
Director, Chenango Valley
Writers' Conference,
Colgate University,
Hamilton, New York
13346-1398
writer@center.colgate.edu

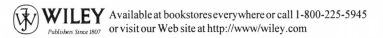

THE MID-ATLANTIC
CREATIVE NONFICTION
SUMMER WRITERS'
CONFERENCE

BALTIMORE, MARYLAND
AUGUST 12-16, 1997

The second annual writers' conference devoted exclusively to the emerging genre of creative nonfiction, featuring distinguished guest writers and faculty.

Includes a unique "Selling What You Write" component.

For a brochure, call 1-800-697-4646 or 410-337-6200
http://www.goucher.edu/~cnf

Goucher College Center for Graduate and Continuing Studies
Co-sponsored by the Creative Nonfiction Foundation

GUEST WRITERS
Tracy Kidder
Tobias Wolff
Gay Talese

CONFERENCE FACULTY
Darcy Frey
Jeanne Marie Laskas
Susan Orlean
Lauren Slater

CONFERENCE DIRECTOR
Lee Gutkind

GOUCHER COLLEGE

Northern Gold
from Alaska Northwest Books™

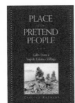

Place of the Pretend People
by Carolyn Kremers

"This book explores what makes any of us authentic."
—Alaska magazine

"She (Kremers) is at her best when creating a scene, giving us a picture of days and nights in modern day Yup'ik society, not paying artificial reverence to the past but rather showing us what exists today."
—Fairbanks Daily News Miner

A Place Beyond
by Nick Jans

"Nick Jans celebrates the Eskimo village of Ambler where he has lived for 17 years earning his living variously as a teacher, basketball coach and big-game guide. Ambler may be isolated, but it's no longer primitive now that oil money has provided electricity, water and sewer, and airport, satellite relays for phone and TV, a clinic and a $2 million school."
—Publishers Weekly

The Last Light Breaking
by Nick Jans

"He writes eloquently of wolves, bears and caribou, and of the stillness and grace of the arctic landscape. ...Jans' insights into Eskimo culture and values ring with authenticity and warmth, and he writes with an unromanticized respect for his fellow villagers."
—Seattle Times

The Last New Land
Edited by Wayne Mergler
With a foreword by John Haines

"This handsome 816-page Alaska anthology collects poetry and prose from 80 writers on the wonders of our 49th state....A hefty, impressive volume."
—The Bloomsbury Review

Look for these titles at your local bookstore or call 800.452.3032

Alaska Northwest Books™, an imprint of Graphic Arts Center Publishing Co.
P.O. Box 10306.Portland.OR.97296-0306